A Guide to Canoe Design and Construction

A Collection of Historical Boat Building Articles on How to Construct Various Types of Canoe

By

Various Authors

British Library Cataloguing-in-Publication Data
A catalogue record for this book is available from
the British Library

Contents

ANY man in the least acquainted with tools can build this canoe. I made my first one when I was twelve and two more when I was sixteen and nineteen respectively. The first one had no sails and only a little cockpit three feet long, so that, while she was good for day cruises and paddling up creeks after snipe and rail birds, you could neither sleep in her nor sail her. The second had a six-foot cockpit and leg-o'-mutton mainsail and jigger. Also a gaudy awning-canvas tent which went over the cockpit, and I had many a glorious cruise in her, sleeping at night in the canoe after hauling her out on the beach and banking sand around her to keep her steady. She had one defect which you should be warned against—she had a kyak bow and stern, little low six-inch oak blocks screwed to the keel at each end, just high enough to take the six ribbands of the frame. Easy to make, but, gee! she was a wet boat in heavy weather! That kyak bow would shoot through every wave like a dagger, and in spite of an eighteen-inch hood over the cockpit for'd, a deluge of sea water would come aft and most of it would stay in the canoe. But she would go like a streak, and when I was seventeen I sailed her across Prince's Bay in a bird of a southeast blow, soaked to the ears with salt spray but cheerful as a clam at high tide. It was some hike, believe me!

I stung another boy with her for $5 and built No. 3, which had a 14-inch bow and 12-inch stern, was fourteen feet long by 32 inches beam. She had lateen-rigged mainsail and jigger, weighed 42 pounds, and was a corking little boat. I had her for ten years and cruised in her for weeks at a time. She finally died of numerous broken ribs, a bunch of kids using her holy bottom as a jumping stand one winter when she was left out in the yard.

Number Four is shown in the accompanying illustrations. She is 16 inches deep at the bow and 14 at the stern, 10 inches amidship, fourteen feet long, 33 inches beam and weighs just 40 pounds, exclusive of her sails. She will cost you $7.00 to build, not including her sails, and for an all-around cruiser is hard to beat, as she will live in water that would drown an open canoe, is a dry, rainproof and mosquito-proof home to sleep in at night, and will sail dozens of miles where you would paddle one.

Most of our writers of boys' books advise building a canvas canoe of barrel hoops. That is conclusive evidence that they never built a canoe in their lives, for of all the material to give you a cranky, unsafe, tippy canoe the barrel hoop is king. The reason is because it is round—just the shape to roll over—and can't be made to hold any other shape. Look at any good Indian model canoe (Morris, White, etc.) and you will see that it is flat-bottomed with a fair round bilge or turn-up from bottom to sides and it is hard to upset because you must submerge one side before the other can come up. Now any kind of a barrel hoop has been steamed round, there is not a flat spot in it anywhere, and to make a canoe even passably steady you want at least 20 inches of flat bottom before curving up over the bilge.

The ideal rib stick is one that will tend to keep flat and yet permit a sharp bend upward at the bilge. There is no wood better for this purpose than black ash, though white will do. Go to any wagonmaker's shop and ask him for a board of black ash about five feet long, an inch thick and five inches wide. He will charge you fifteen cents for it. Take it to the nearest wood-working mill and get them to rip it up for you into strips one-eighth inch thick. You will get some twenty canoe ribs out of the board. While at the mill ask to see their No. 1 spruce stock. Tell them you want one board, planed both sides, sixteen feet long, free from knots. Have this ripped up into strips a quarter-inch thick until you have sixteen of them. You will have half your board still left and from it you will have two ¾-inch pieces ripped off and two 2-inch. Next, you want a piece of 2-inch by 3-inch white oak six feet long, two pieces of ⅞-inch half-round yellow pine moulding sixteen feet long, two pieces ½-inch quarter-round ditto and one piece 2½ x ½-inch beaded white pine for a cockpit coaming. Have them all wrapped up into a bundle, pay your mill bill, which should be about two dollars, and march home with the entire material for your canoe frame on your shoulder. The bundle will weigh thirty pounds.

Arrived home the first thing to do is to set to work at that stick of 2 by 3-inch white oak, for out of it you make the stem and stern knees. From the drawings herewith you will get the angles for bow and stern pieces. Saw across the top of the stick at this angle and again a parallel cut 14 inches from the top. Saw it straight across 9 inches further on and take the two pieces so obtained and stand the 14-inch piece up on the other. You will at once see that you have, roughly, the bow knee. Draw the curve of the bow on both pieces of wood and saw off the superfluous wood beyond the curve. You now must work both pieces into triangular shape and the best tool to do it with is a camp axe. Your stem should be half an inch thick at the extreme front so as to give room to screw on a brass stem-band, so draw two lines ½-inch apart down the center of the front face of the blocks. Hew from these lines back to the rear corners with your axe until you have dubbed the stem and keel-piece roughly triangular in cross section and finish smooth with a plane. Now nail the stem to the keel-piece and you are ready to fit the deadwood, the triangular piece which holds both of them together. Take off the angle for this on a piece of paper from your already assembled stem and keel-piece and transfer the angle to your piece of oak stick, being careful to saw out the block with true cuts square across.

If well done the deadwood block will fit snugly and you can screw it home with 2½-inch, No. 14 iron screws into stem and keel-piece. Work over the deadwood block until you get a true fit, as this is what takes the shock if you ram anything (and

you're always ramming things on a canoe cruise).
Drill screw-holes in the deadwood a little larger
than the screws and just a little smaller than
these in the back of stem and keel-piece. The bow
knee is now done and the stern is made the same
way. The next job will be to cut a shallow ⅛-inch
rabbet on stem and stern and keel-piece to take
the canvas, and six notches on a side for the ends
of the ribbands. The top notches must be deep
enough to take two ribbands one on top of the
other, ½ inch deep. Now saw out the places in
both stem and stern keel blocks to take keelson
and keel, as shown in the working drawings, and
the long job on stem and stern knees is done.

The canoe will go ahead with a rush from now
on. Take one of your ¾-inch strips and cut it
13 feet long for a keelson. Cut a shallow notch
in the center ⅛-inch by 1 inch and cut one like it
at every foot each way to within one foot from
each end. Turn the notches down and screw on
the stern and stem knees at each end of the keelson. Follow with a ribband nailed along under
the keelson and of the same length, and then fit
the keel, rockering it 1½ inches each way and
screwing from underneath to the keelson with long
3-inch screws or bolts. By rockering is meant
tapering along the under side of the keel, which is

CANOEING AND CRUISING

made out of one of your 2-inch spruce strips and
should taper down to ½-inch deep at each end,
beginning five feet from the end. The job is
best done with a hatchet and finished to a line
with the plane.

Now you are ready for the center mould. Make
it of box boards as shown in the illustrations and
set up over the middle notch in the keelson. Now
take the first of your ash ribs, slip it through the
middle notch and bend it snugly around the mould
board, tying together across the top with a piece
of string so that the rib cannot fly out straight
again. Now take four ribbands, slip them in pairs
over the ends of the mid-rib, bend them in at bow
and stern and nail them temporarily over their
notches with thin brads. Do not cut them off until everything else is done, as there will be a lot
of taking up and letting out before the bottom is
even and smooth. Put on all the other ribbands,
five on a side, spacing them evenly along the mid-
rib and tacking them in place by brads driven
through ribband and rib into the edge of the mould
board. Tack them temporarily over their notches
at stem and stern, letting each ribband take its
natural curve.

You are now ready for the ribs, only the last
two of which at each end will have to be steamed.

7

DECKED CRUISING CANOES

Beginning each side of the mid-rib, shove in a rib down between the two ribbands of the gunwale, through the notch under the keelson and up between the opposite pair of gunwale ribbands. Tack it with a brad half-driven through the keelson and rib and then push down the ends of the rib on each side until you get a true flat, almost like that of the mid-rib with almost as sharp a bend at the bilge. Lash tight with twine around the gunwale. You will also have to lash the mouldboard down, as the tendency of the ash rib is to raise it and make your bottom not flat and safe but round and cranky. Put in the other ribs the same way, working in pairs towards bow and stern, always trying to have each curve a little less than the one before it and keeping them as flat across the keelson as possible. The last two will have to be steamed, easily done by simply wrapping a soaking towel of scalding water about the rib and letting it stand ten minutes while you drip on more steaming water from the tea kettle.

The ribs just behind the stem and stern bend up from the keel so sharply that they simply *must* break, so, to put them in, whittle a block to shape and screw it down on the keelson, cut the rib in two and screw the lower ends of it to the block.

CANOEING AND CRUISING

Tie the ribs to the ribbands wherever they cross and then turn the canoe frame over. You will find it all hills and valleys—flat spot here, a bulge there, two halves of the same rib uneven, a lop-sided place somewhere else. What it needs is patient adjustment, shoving down the end of a rib in one place to give her more bilge, letting it up somewhere else, pulling a ribband in a little flatter or letting it out a bit, but finally the whole bottom will come out smooth and fair and is ready to rivet.

Whether to use copper rivets or clinched copper nails I leave to you. All my canoes except this last one were done with 2d copper nails clinched inside and all were staunch and strong. In this one I used rivets (No. 1—⅞-inch long) but it was a tedious job as they all had to have holes drilled for them, a shallow countersink made to sink the rivet-head flush with the ribband, and the little burrs are most exasperating to keep on while you are hammering over the rivet head. With copper nails it is just a drill hole with the brad awl, insert the nail and clinch over. However, do them all but the gunwale, which will be all out of shape from the pressure of the rib ends, and then untie your twine and adjust the gunwale to get a fair and pretty sheer. Secure with brass screws and cut off the rib ends flush with the gunwale. You will find that the strain of the ribs on the ribbands has pulled both your stem and stern knee out of shape so that ugly cracks show around the deadwood block. You now pull out all those temporary brads in the ribband ends and free the stem and stern. Close up the cracks snugly with a few taps of the hammer and then put back the ribbands, beginning with the gunwales and cutting each off to exactly fit in its notch. Secure with ¾-inch brass screws, two to the notch.

The frame is now done and should weigh 24 pounds. Next you go in for the deck framing. At bow and stern insert the triangular white pine boards called breasthooks. Cut a 1½-inch hole for the mainmast step and cut out an oak block with a 1-inch round cup drilled in it for a footstep for the mainmast and secure it to the bow deadwood, giving the mainmast a pretty "rake" or lean aft. Now for the cockpit. If you are going to sleep in her it ought to be six feet long, so the cross-braces must go at the third rib each way from mid-rib. Make these cross-pieces out of your 2-inch spruce strip, sawing them so as to pitch an inch each way from the center. Cut a notch for the deck ridge piece and then put in your braces with 1½-inch brass screws driven into their

CANOEING AND CRUISING

ends through the gunwale. At the same time take
out the mould board as you no longer need it.
Next get out your ridge pieces of the 2-inch spruce
strip, planing them to the ridge along the top surface and fitting them into notches in the cross-
braces and breasthooks at bow and stern. The
rear ridge piece wants a 1½-inch hole cut in it
for the jigger mast step, so you had better nail
reinforcing strips on each side where this hole
goes through. The cockpit coaming should go
about three inches from the gunwale, parallel to
it, so lay off the three inches on each side on the
cross-braces. Then cut from your 2½-inch white
pine beaded cockpit coaming two pieces of the
same length as between the marks and screw them
to the cross-braces, allowing the beading to just
project above the cross-brace. To fit the coaming sides, measure off two lengths a little longer
than you need, cut a spreader six inches shorter
than the inside measurement from gunwale at
the mid-rib and bend the two coaming sides around
this spreader, held fast with a loop of rope at each
end. Pick up this frame and put it on the canoe
and saw off the coaming ends so that they will exactly fit between the cross-braces, slip them into
place and secure with blocks, besides nailing with
brads to the cockpit end pieces. At each rib you

will now need a small block between gunwale and cockpit coaming secured by 1½-inch brass screws through the gunwale and 1-inch screws through the coaming. When all are in, the spreader can be knocked out and the canoe frame is ready for the canvas and will weigh 28 pounds.

To make the canvas lie smoothly a last job will be to plane the edges of the ribbands round and smooth so that sharp rib edges will not make the canoe look like the ribs of a starved dog. Get ten yards of 10-oz. duck canvas (20 cents a yard). It will weigh 100 oz. or a little over 6 lbs. Cut it in half and have the two 5-yard pieces sewed together on the sewing machine along the blue line overlap mark. Now take off the keel and lay this seam along the keelson ribband, tacking it here and there with 4-oz. copper tacks. Fold the canvas up over bow and stern and tack here and there to the gunwale. Cut off the surplus all around and save all of it, for there is enough for both bow and stern deck and the strips of deck outside the coaming. Now stretch and tack on the canvas, working each way from the center, but do not drive the tacks home nor use more than one every four inches. At the point where the stem and stern rabbet crosses the crack in the bow and stern knee, drill a half-inch hole and drive

in a soft white pine plug called a stopwater. Next
daub the whole rabbet over with white lead paste
and stretch the canvas tight into the rabbet, tacking close together. Now work back along the gunwale towards the mid-rib, stretching the canvas
as tight as you can, tacking every two inches and
being sure to work on opposite sides of the canoe
alternately. In spite of all your care there will
probably be a gather or pucker in the canvas
amidships, but do not let this worry you, simply
slit it four inches down from the gunwale and
sew up the overlap. Take your left-over canvas
and get out the bow and stern decks, tacking them
over the side of the gunwales. You will also find
that the original pieces of canvas cut off along
the side when reversed will exactly fit along the
coaming. Tack them to it, stretch taut over the
gunwale and trim off all the hangover.

The canoe is now ready for paint and weighs
34 pounds. I have tried all kinds of ways to reduce the paint weight and also its cost. On this
last canoe I tried one coat of shellac and two of
Sherwin-Williams willow green canoe varnish.
Total paint bill $3.00, total weight 6 pounds. On
the whole the cheapest and best was that on
Waterat III, two coats of white lead paint and a
finish of any color preferred. Avoid varnishes

and shellacs and save expense. You ought to come out under $2.00 cost and 8 pounds weight. After the paint is on, put your ⅞-inch yellow pine half-round moulding along your gunwales, and the ½-inch quarter-round beading around the cockpit. Give these two coats of varnish and you are ready to go at your rigging.

I have tried leg-o'-mutton, lateen, and battened leg-o'-mutton or Canadian Club, and on the whole I prefer the latter. The leg-o'-mutton is the simplest, but it has long spars impossible to stow in the canoe, and its baggy leach makes it slow sailing. The lateen also has long spars, but the draft is excellent and fast. It is, however, hard to reef. *Waterat IV*, my latest canoe, has the battened leg-o'-mutton shown in the illustrations. It is a top-heavy, dangerous rig in large sizes for any but first-class canoe sailors, and the amount of canvas shown in the photographs is "man's sized." Sailing the little witch in a squally breeze is some busy occupation! However, by making the boom of the mainsail two feet shorter and all the rest of the measurements in like proportion (the actual dimensions as given in the sail plan drawing) a very good safe rig is had. The best sail-cloth is American Drilling, 14 cents a yard, and you will want about eight yards. To lay out a sail, choose a level spot on the lawn and stake out the sail according to the dimensions given, cocking the boom up 18 inches above a right angle and setting the gaff up nearly straight, allowing just room for a block between it and the mast head. Join the stakes with twine and spread out the canvas under the twine outline, always laying it parallel to the leach or after-edge of the sail. Hem it all around and put in grommets every foot along the boom, gaff and luff. To put in the batten, fold over a pocket in the sail just large enough to pass a ¼-inch by 1-inch strip of spruce ribband and sew a seam along both edges of the pocket on the sewing machine. To make the spars you can buy 1½-inch and 1¼-inch round spruce sticks 14 feet long at any sash-and-door mill for about 25 cents apiece and they will save you much weary planing as all they need is tapering at the ends. The masts are of 1½-inch stock, booms and gaffs 1¼-inch. For gaff jaws you can buy a regular brass canoe gaff jaw and bend it over at the right angle to grip the mast when the gaff is up. You will need 5 two-inch mast rings for the luffs of mainsail and mizzen, and don't forget to grease the mast with tallow candle or slush. Four brass cleats and four pulley blocks complete your running rigging. Two pulley blocks are for the halliards at main and mizzen mast heads, one on the deck for a main halliard fair-leader and one on the rudder-head for the mizzen sheet.

For extras, first of all, a bottom grid. Cut up what you have left of the ribband stock into 6-foot lengths and tie them to the ribs in the cockpit along between the ribbands. Otherwise your toes will be digging into the canvas bottom all the time, making unsightly dents in it. Another way is to tie in a sheet of oilcloth or heavy canvas, which will serve to keep your feet off the bottom. You want two canoe paddles, a big double blade with drip cups, and a little single-blade pudding-stick for working in narrow creeks, frogging, etc. The latter may be 30 inches long by 5 inches wide and you saw and whittle it out of a white pine board. Then you want a cockpit tent to have the best fun in a canoe. Get six yards of 8-ounce duck canvas. Make a rope frame with two spreaders the same size as your cockpit and stretch the rope frame between main and mizzen masts 30 inches above the cockpit. Over this spread your canvas, cutting and pinning until you have a little rectangular house over the cockpit, and have it sewed up on the machine. Cut a door in one side and fill with mosquito netting. Put in staples in the cockpit leading along the sides and grommets in the bottom hem of the tent to match the staples. Take along a browse bag and fill it with leaves or sage at night, and, my word for it, you will sleep in that mosquito-proof, rain-proof and damp-proof canoe-house like a major!

THE day of sail canoeing seems to have gone out of vogue of late, giving place to the light, open Indian type of canoe. Time was when one could go to the far ends of the earth in the canvas-covered cruising canoe or its heavier wooden counterpart, though I always preferred the former. I see no good reason for this change, and hope that these chapters on the canvas cruiser will do something to revive a most interesting type of long-distance canoeing. As a matter of fact you can build a very serviceable canvas canoe with spruce and ash framing and ten-ounce duck skin which will not weigh over thirty-five pounds. Nessmuk, who navigated in the lightest wooden canoes in the world, weighing but 11 lbs., seemed to think that canvas canoes gained in weight with age and were limp, logy, and non-floating when awash. As a matter of fact he spoke from hearsay on this matter and never gave the canvas canoe a chance. Far from being logy it is as taut and spruce a craft as floats, lively and safe in seaways that would have held Nessmuk's ten-foot open canoe helplessly wind-bound, and, if you upset, which may happen if some accident like a jamming rudder befalls you, she will fill to the brim and yet carry your weight nicely, while you kick her ashore, or, if the seas are not too choppy, you can bail her out from the water alongside, crawl in over the stern and go your ways rejoicing. I have done both and I *know*. And she is the only solution of the mosquito problem in a cruise along the great Atlantic bays, such as the one to Currituck Sound and back via inside route from New York. For the canvas cruising canoe is the one impervious sleeping resort—where marsh mosquitoes abound. Its tent is virtually a little rectangular house over the cockpit, and is provided with a mosquito blind inside the flap. When you retire for the night, not only is the tent buttoned firmly to the cockpit all around, but the bottom edge of the mosquito bar is also. You gather a few armfuls of sage for bedding, strew them in the bottom of the canoe, pile sand around her as she lies up the beach, step in the two masts and guy the tent between them, leading out to pegs on the beach,—and the ravenous horde of stingarees outside can sample the tent or the canvas deck, or the canoe bottom, to their heart's content for all you care. In making a canoe tent, ordinary sober whites and drabs seem out of keeping with such a gay bird as the canoe has been proving herself to be all day long. I always prefer something loud in awning effects, broad, noisy stripes that are blatantly aggressive on the color-scheme of the surrounding scenery. These stripes should go vertically, and four feet high is plenty. The tent should be just the length and width of your cockpit, which will be about 2 feet wide by 6 feet long. To make it, sew two strips of yard-wide awning duck together, hemming across the ends. This piece will give you both sides and the top. Get out two more strips a little over two feet wide and five inches longer than the height of the tent. Hem at the bottom and sew to the other piece of canvas, making the ends of the tent. Each of these ends will now have two five-inch flaps sticking up above the tent top. Get two spreaders (stout sticks, like broom handles) and sew these flaps around them, sewing the leftover edge inside the top of the tent at the ends with a double seam. Run in two bolt ropes of ⅛-inch white cotton rope inside the tent from one stick to the other, and sew it to the canvas every foot, or overstitch it to it all along its length. Bend on a bridle to each of the sticks and put in grommets every foot along the bottom of the tent. To set up:—Run the canoe up on the beach, pile sand around her, step the main and mizzen masts furled, lead out guy-ropes for bridles of the fore and aft spreader-sticks of the tent and guy to pegs in the sand. Use the main and mizzen sheets for side guys. Along the outside of your cockpit should be a row of brass awning buttons or hooks, which you can get from any ship chandlery, and you now snap the grommets over these hooks and the tent is up. For doors you simply leave about three feet of the middle seam on each side unsewed, and sew to the edges of the flap thus formed a loose fold of green mosquito netting of the strong linen kind, that they use for salt water mosquito bars. This arrangement allows you to pin back one flap and get the air, the opening being covered by the mosquito bar. As the rest of the canoe is mosquito proof this bar will ensure you a good night's sleep, no matter how mosquitoey the country, and in the day time along its Atlantic marshes the mosquitoes are generally at peace with the world. The canoe tent is good and comfortable for mid-summer camping, and is insect and snake-proof, besides giving the maximum of comfort with the least browse, since its circular shape goes in very well with the contours of one's body. I have slept

in them for weeks, and have even tried it off shore
at anchor, but this is apt to end rather moistly
as you never know, when you drift off to sleep,
what the weather is going to do during the night.

Nessmuk's "pudding stick" or auxiliary paddle
I have tried and found good. Get a piece of
⅞-inch by 4-inch clear spruce about two feet
long, and whittle from it a miniature paddle with
a seven-inch blade 4 inches wide. Tie it to a rib
of the canoe with a bit of twine so you can drop
it any time.

It is very useful when working up salt creeks
after rail, snipe or reed birds. Hold the shotgun
in one hand and maneuver her along with the pudding-stick in the other. If a shot offers, drop the
stick alongside while you attend to fresh fowl for
the larder.

A 3½- or 4-pound folding galvanized anchor,
costing about $1.50, is a necessity; also a small
bow chock on each side of the stem, as there will
come times when you will simply *have* to lie to,
when paddling is impossible against head seas.
You can't do anything with her without the bow
chocks unless you perform the delicate maneuver
of crawling out and tying your anchor-line to the
stem ring. The anchor is also handy for fishing

or resting for lunch in the middle of a long traverse.

I do not advise a folding centerboard for a canvas canoe. They are a necessity on the larger wooden cruising canoes, but the little fellow is easy to keep on a level keel and is in fact a boy's paradise in all kinds of blows, so that a good 2½-inch or 3-inch yellow pine keel the entire length of the canoe will keep her from making leeway quite as well as anything of a folding nature. Besides, the smallest of these made is 24 inches long and requires about three inches of flat keel to screw to. A good brass drop rudder is, however, a luxury not to be despised. You can buy these at more or less fancy prices, compared to the cost of building the canoe (about the same money), but you can make one for less than a dollar. Get a piece of half-inch brass pipe 16 inches long and slot its lower end with a hack-saw. Spread the slot to pass a 1-16-inch brass rudder plate. Cut this out, of the conventional round-end rudder shape, 8 inches long by approximately six inches broad. Pin near bottom with ¼-inch brass bolt. Drill two 3/16-inch holes in the back of the pipe to receive the rudder hangers, which are stout brass awning hooks screwed into the stern-post and left upside down. They have just the right slope to allow the rudder to be easily shipped. Finish the rudder by filing a flat at the top to receive the yoke, which should have an eye in the bottom to pass the twine for lowering and raising the rudder. The only other hardware you will need is a jam cleat for the rudder line, two for the main sheet inside the cockpit, and one on the bow deck for the anchor. Halliard cleats are best on deck screwed to the main deck carline. So equipped you will find a canvas canoe trip one of the most enjoyable cruises you ever undertook.

I propose to add here a foot-note on centerboards which has been several years in the making. Leeboards are objectionable as being clumsy and landlubberly; I have always preferred a fixed keel. This latter will, however, not do much towards minimizing your leeward drift when sailing closehauled, so I have schemed much for some sort of canoe centerboard for canvas sail canoes.

Of course the first thing to be investigated was the folding metal fan centerboard, used on wooden sailing canoes. These run from 24 to 40 inches long and, even in galvanized iron cost $8, or more than the cost of the canoe; but that is not its worst defect. The width of three or more inches required by the base of the folding centerboard trunk puts it out of the question for attaching to a ⅞-inch keelson. If I were building a larger *Waterat* of, say, 17 feet L. W. L., intended mainly for sailing purposes, I would make the keel of 5-inch stock, fining down to 1 inch at stem and stern and riveting my ribs across it inside. With this keel there would be plenty of room to screw down the trunk of the folding board, and I am sure that such a cruiser for two men in salt water or lake country would be nearly ideal, for she could carry a lot of sail, would be much lighter than the wooden cruising canoe, and therefore paddle more easily, and it was the bugbear of this tedious and laborious paddling that eventually led to the downfall of the popularity of the wooden sailing canoe.

My cogitations on centerboards for the *Waterats*, as built, led to the design of a thin wooden trunk of shape to take a 12 x 36 x ⅛-inch brass dagger centerboard. This board was to be lined inside with canvas, the lips of which were to be brought out and tacked over the canvas on the keel, thus making a watertight canvas surface inside the trunk, for it is obvious that a plain wooden trunk would surely leak because of the joint between keelson and keel which cannot be got at to calk. By lining the trunk with canvas this difficulty is obviated. To construct such a board, cut a slot through keel, keelson and ridge timber of upper forward deck ⅜ x 12 inches. Let in two uprights of ½ x 1-inch oak, necked down to ⅜ inch where they pass through keel and upper ridge timber, and screw these into place at each end of the slots, setting the joint in white lead paste. Now screw to each side of these uprights the sideboards of the trunk, with their canvas inside facings already stuck fast on them by painting down with several coats of paint. These facings should have about three inches of free canvas along their lower edges, which canvas is pulled down through the slot in keel and keelson and brought around outside the canoe, where they are pulled smooth and flat and tacked outside the main canvas skin of the canoe with copper tacks set close together and liberally doped with white lead paste. This construction will give you a watertight, canvas-lined centerboard trunk suitable for a narrow dagger-type centerboard of ⅛-inch brass with a wooden stop or top, which board is to be shoved down through the slot in the upper forward deck, which is the upper end of your trunk.

The above design is easily put in while building the canoe, and, even for a built one, simply involves taking off the forward upper deck so as to get at the work. As *Waterat IV* was wanted up at the June encampment of the Camp Fire Club and I was too busy to attempt any extensive work on the canoe that year, I built on her a detachable keelboard, put on and taken off with wing nuts like a set of leeboards as we used to do with keel rowboats. All you needed was a piece of 8x⅞-inch yellow pine about three feet long, and two ¼-inch carriage bolts 2½ inches long with wing nuts. It did not take half an hour to put this scheme into execution. I sawed a slant fore and aft on the keelboard, so that in running aground or striking anything submerged I would not be brought up all standing and have something ripped loose. Two carriage bolts were driven through, about eight inches from either end of the keelboard; the holes for them were marked on the 2½-inch keel (which, you will remember, is permanently secured to the bottom of the *Waterat* models), and, before putting her overboard, the carriage bolts of the keelboard were shoved through these holes in my keel and secured fast with the two wing nuts. Other sailors had leeboards; I had a keelboard! and, for a long time, they were mystified as to what kept the *Waterat* so well up into the eye of the wind with no visible lee-board gear.

BUILDING A CANOE.

S O you think you would like to build your own canoe? Of course you do, or you wouldn't be reading this book.

Probably the first thing you did when you opened it was to look at the plans and drawings, and it is quite possible that your first reaction was that building a boat wasn't quite so simple as you had imagined.

Well, it isn't very difficult if you go the right way about it, but never forget that it is not a job to be undertaken lightly. Your life may depend upon the skill and honesty with which you have performed your task, and you must resolve to follow the instructions contained in these pages implicitly. Only when you have followed out these plans and have gained some experience of handling the resulting craft will you be qualified to modify any of the constructional details which follow.

This may seem an unnecessary warning, but I have known young chaps take the trouble to consult me on the feasibility of doing this or that thing, and because they had really made up their minds as to what they wanted to do before they came to see me, the fact that my advice did not fit in with their intentions did not prevent them from learning for themselves. Fortunately all of them have survived to admit that beginner's luck alone enabled them to get away with it.

The canoe described in these pages was designed by my collaborator, a canoeist who has two sons, both of whom

28

have been keen canoeists since their teens. He designed it specially to appeal to the constructive streak in every boy and that it can be made successfully by the average boy has been proved by the designer and is borne out by the illustrations which appear in these pages.

As a canoe, it is strong, light and easy to handle, and I have yet to see its equal for this type of rigid, canvas-covered canoe. Officially, it is described as a 16 ft. 0 ins. canvas covered Hard Chine Kayak.

Let us look at the plans together, before we go any further. We can then size up the job and see what we are up against.

You will see from Sheet 1 that the canoe consists of a keel on which are fixed seven shaped frames, the hull and deck components being attached to these. A canvas covering makes the whole thing watertight.

That sounds pretty flimsy, but the description only deals with the broad outline. The art of making a canoe which is going to be a success comes in the introduction of various features which will be described. Also, there are one or two definitions which you may not have come across before.

Before turning to Sheet 2, just let me deal with the definitions. You will notice that the canoe has two keels, described as a keel and a false keel. The real keel is there to perform the same functions as the keel of any ship. It is part of the ship, and without it the canoe would fall to pieces. The false keel is screwed to the real keel, underneath the real keel, and is there to protect the bottom of the canoe when grounding or when contact is accidentally made with some underwater hazard. It is screwed on after the canvas covering has been fixed in position.

You will notice other strips of wood fastened to the bottom of the canoe. These are the rubbing strips and their function is the same as that of the false keel. They are fastened to

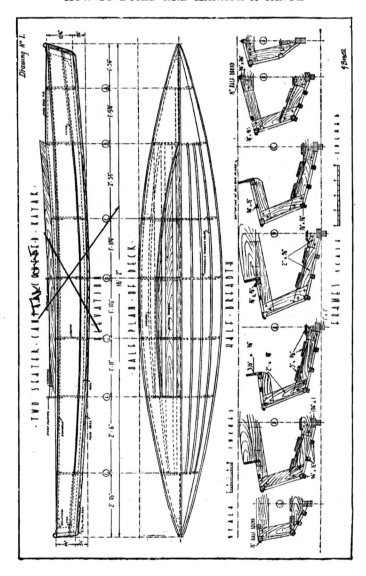

the stringers, as the longitudinal strips of wood which constitute the ribs of the craft are called.

Now for a look at the deck of the canoe. Gunwales are familiar to everyone, and might be defined as the wooden strips which form the upper outline of the canoe The coaming is the wall raised round the cockpit which prevents watei from coming in. The carlines may not be so familiar. They are to the upper deck what the stringers are to the bottom of the canoe. Rubbing strips are also fastened to the gunwales.

The function of the stretcher is implied by its name, and it is incorporated into the construction of Frame D.

The chines are longitudinal strips of wood running at the part of the canoe where the sides may be said to end and the bottom commence. They are readily recognisable on the plans of the frames because they are the only pentagonal pieces of wood in the craft. They acquire this shape as the result of a chamfer which is carried out after they have been fixed in position, to make them harmonise with the general lines of the craft.

The burden boards are the floor boards of the cockpit and are not fixed to the frames, with the exception of the centre board which extends from Frame A to Frame G and is screwed to each frame.

The breasthooks are pieces of wood, triangular in shape, to which are fixed the stem and the stern, and to which the gunwales converge and are fixed.

The knees are triangular shaped pieces of wood fixed to the stem and the stern and the keel. They form a firm angle of wood, holding the keel rigidly to the stem and stern pieces.

So much for the definitions. Now turn to the second sheet and let us have a look at those features which go to make a successful canoe. You will see on the frame plans how the vital parts of the canoe are protected by the rubbing strips

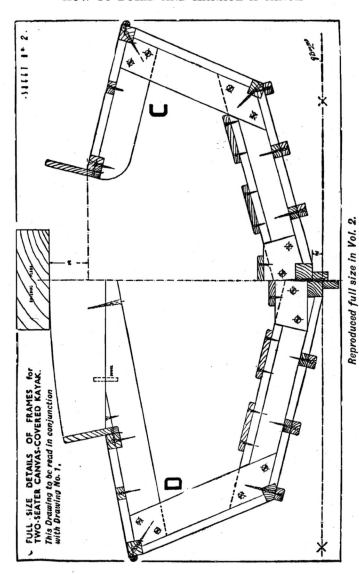

FULL SIZE DETAILS OF FRAMES for TWO-SEATER CANVAS-COVERED KAYAK. This Drawing to be read in conjunction with Drawing No. 1.

Reproduced full size in Vol. 2.

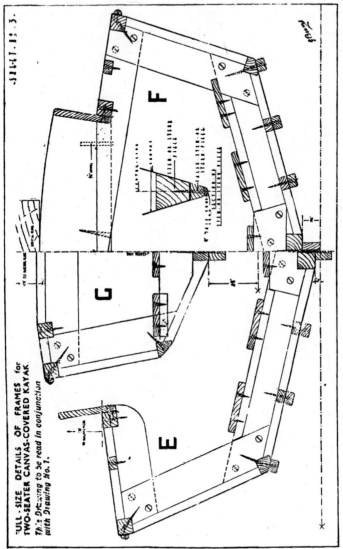

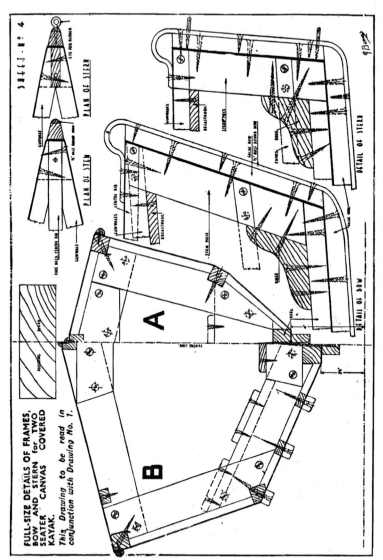

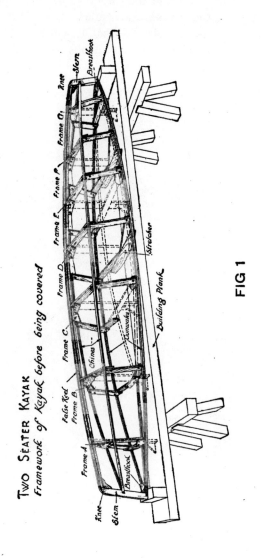

TWO SEATER KAYAK
Framework of Kayak before being covered

FIG 1

which are fixed outside the canvas at all those points which
have to bear the stresses and strains. There is the protection
round the gunwales, also, so that it will be seen that every
part of the hull which is in continuous contact with the water

FIG 2

is protected by what we might describe as wooden armour,
which can be replaced if damaged or worn out.

One point about the plans of the frames may puzzle you.

You will notice that the burden boards are screwed to a piece of wood and not to the frames, with the exception of the centre burden board, which *is* screwed to the frames. This piece of

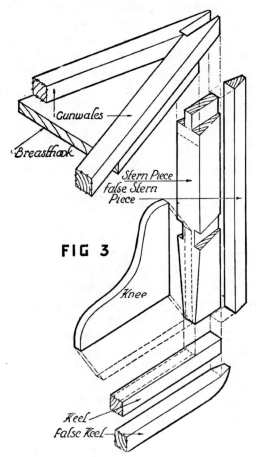

Gunwales

Breasthook

Stern Piece
False Stern
Piece

FIG 3

Knee

Keel
False Keel

wood is not fastened to anything else and the object of it is to keep the burden boards in position. The piece of wood, fitting over the woodwork of the frames, prevents the burden boards from shifting about.

Turning to Sheet 3, you will see that further strengthening for the canoe is provided by a false stern piece, while Sheet 4, gives you full constructional details of the bow and stern pieces.

If you have any remaining difficulty in understanding anything connected with the plans, a glance at Fig. 1, which depicts the skeleton of the canoe in perspective, should smooth away your doubts.

Figs. 2 and 3 show the constructional details of the stern piece.

We are now ready to describe the order of construction in detail.

Before the actual building of the canoe is commenced, a number of parts can be made and finished as complete units. All the frames, the stem and stern pieces, the knees and the breasthooks, can be made separately.

The frames should be made first. A study of the full-size plans will show you how each is constructed. Start by marking off the various parts on the timber, and when these have been cut, screw them together with brass screws. If you pin down the full-size drawing on a flat surface, you can lay the pieces on the drawing while you screw them up.

The stretcher which forms the top of Frame D, and the stern coaming on Frame F, are dowelled on to the top member of the respective frames at the points where the wood is too deep for a screw.

When all the frames are complete, notches must be cut to receive the keel, gunwales and chines, and you must not attempt to cut these notches until the frames are assembled.

The reason for this is that for each piece to be cut with the notches in it means very fine working, and a slight error in each piece will be multiplied: whereas, if the notch is cut after the frame has been screwed together you can cut the notches in the two pieces at once.

In one of the first canoes to be built to the specifications described in this book the builder tried the plan of cutting the notches in each piece and got himself into an awful mess. When we showed him how to cut the notches after the frames had been put together he managed alright.

Another point easily overlooked is that some of the notches in the frames near the bow and stern require to be cut on the splay. A glance at the plan will show this to be so.

The stem and stern pieces are tapered and must have rebates or grooves cut in them to take the ends of the gunwales and chines. The knees can be fixed to the stem and stern pieces when they are made, but the breasthooks, when made, are not fitted at this stage.

No longitudinal members should be cut to dead length until the frames are erected on the building plank.

BUILDING THE CANOE.

The first thing required is a plank on which to build the canoe. The most useful size is a plank six inches wide and two inches deep, but whatever you can get near this size will do, so long as the piece of wood is about a foot longer than the proposed canoe.

The best way to arrange the "stocks" is to fix the plank on supports firmly to the floor. Take care to see that it is perfectly rigid, level and straight, for on this depends the truth of the canoe. Fig. 1, will give you the idea of how to set the plank up. If you haven't got trestles you can substitute boxes, of course, so long as the resulting erection is rigid, level and straight.

Having fixed up the stocks, the next thing to do is to mark off on the plank the positions of the frames, which will then be fixed to it by means of brackets. Metal shelf brackets are quite suitable, but if you prefer it you can use triangles of wood screwed to the plank and to the frames, or to a temporary piece of wood which in turn is fixed to the frame. Another glance at Fig. 1 will make this clear.

The canoe is built bottom upwards, and the first frames to be fixed will be the two end ones A and G. Be careful to see that you fix these frames vertically, square to the plank and the correct distance above it. Then fix the intermediate frames, B, C, D, E and F.

Having fixed all the frames, the next thing is to ensure that they are in true alignment. If you stretch a string taut between the two end frames from the centre lines already marked on them, this will provide a guide on which the centre line of each frame can be lined up. This string must be fixed between the two end frames *before* the intermediate ones are fixed, otherwise, if any of them are not in their correct position, it will be a case of re-fixing after the string is stretched. In other words the string will act as a check instead of a guide unless you fix it before fixing the intermediate frames. Furthermore, human nature being what it is, if a frame is not in its right position to begin with, the builder may say to himself that it is only a bit out, and that it won't matter, The result will be to spoil the curve of the canoe, and the resulting kink in the gunwales will be a source of weakness.

With regard to the varying distances above the plank at which the frames should be fixed, you will find these distances marked on the full-sized drawings.

When the stem and stern pieces have been fixed to the keel by means of the knees, drop the keel into the slots in the frames and fix it to them with screws. The stem and stern pieces can be fixed to the building plank by temporary brackets.

The gunwales are fixed next. It is advisable to leave the

gunwales a little longer than required, and only fix them temporarily to the frames. Commence by screwing the gunwale to frame D, then to E and C. Then fix the gunwale on the opposite side to the same frames. Next fix the gunwale to frames B and F, afterwards fixing the other gunwale to the same frames. Then fix to A and G, and finish by fixing the other gunwale to A and G. Use smaller screws than those which will be used to fix the gunwales permanently.

The two gunwales will now be held firmly in their correct positions and you can mark off the ends for cutting to the correct length and also for fitting into the rebates prepared in the stem and stern. The next step is to remove both gunwales, taking out the screws alternately on both sides. This is to prevent the natural spring in the wood from straining one side of the canoe. Then trim the ends to the required length, afterwards replacing the gunwales. This time you fix them in position with the correct size screws, and it is still important to observe the same order as before for putting in the screws.

Next screw the ends of the gunwales to the breasthooks, and fix the ends at the stern to the stern piece. At the bow the gunwales will be fixed to the member running from the cockpit to the bow, but this member cannot be fixed at this stage.

Let me emphasize again that you must not attempt completely to fix or remove one gunwale. You must always work on alternate sides, otherwise distortion will take place and the result will be what is known as a crank-built craft.

We are now ready to fix the chines, which are put on in a similar manner, being first fixed in position, the length marked off, then removed and the ends trimmed, being finally refixed. Then it is necessary to plane a chamfer so that the awkward angle presented by the exposed portion of the chines is smoothed away to conform to the general lines of the hull.

After the chines comes the turn of the stringers, which should now be fixed to the frames. The stringers not only serve to strengthen the bottom of the craft and to withstand the upward pressure of the water, but also as something solid to which to screw the rubbing strips which are added to protect the canvas.

It is important that the heads of all screws should be slightly countersunk, so that there will be no chance of them chafing the canvas which is the next job to which we have to turn our attention.

The fixing of the canvas is a job which needs to be done painstakingly, if the result is going to look nice. How the canvas is fitted depends on the width of the material used. The best job is obtained by the use of canvas wide enough to cover the whole canoe in one piece, and the directions which follow are written on the assumption that such a piece of canvas is going to be used.

You start by laying the canvas over the framework with the centre of the material lying along the keel. Then, using $\frac{3}{8}$ in. copper tacks, start at the centre and, working outwards to the ends, tack at 6 in. intervals along the keel until you reach the point where the keel commences to rise. Then go back to the middle of the canoe and tack the canvas to the gunwales, straining the material as you go. Make quite sure that no wrinkles are left and then tack a foot or so on one side, and then repeat the process on the other side. Don't drive the tacks right home, as it may be necessary to remove one here and there.

From the points where the canvas has been tacked to the keel, to the bow and stern, the material will have to be cut. Strain the canvas over the keel and gunwale on one side of the canoe at the bow and stern. When all the wrinkles have been removed and the canvas is tight all over, the material can be tacked at one-inch intervals along the keel and gun-wales. The surplus can be cut off at the keel at the point where you have had to cut the material. Turn the raw edge under and tack it to the side of the keel.

The pieces on the other side of the canoe can now be trimmed off, leaving enough to be turned under one inch along the keel, as shown in Fig. 2.

The bow and stern are treated in the same manner: the one side being taken round the bow, or the stern, as the case may be, and tacked to the side. The other side is brought round, turned under one inch and tacked at intervals of one inch.

Wherever you have to lap canvas the joint must have a coat of white lead applied before the top piece is tacked down. This is to ensure a watertight joint.

The canvas can now be given a good coat of paint, which must contain plenty of linseed oil. Leave it to dry thoroughly, a process which may take two or three days.

When dry the false keel, and the bow and stern pieces can be fixed after a good coat of white lead has been applied. The final tightening of the fixing screws will squeeze out the surplus, which can be scraped off and used again.

Then fix the rubbing strips in a similar manner. The screws will pull the strips up tight to the stringers. The whole canoe can now be given a further coat of oil paint and when this is perfectly dry we are ready for the "launch".

This is effected by removing the canoe from the building plank. The brackets, and the temporary pieces of wood used to fix the brackets to the frames are taken out, and the canoe, now the right way up, should be given its first coat of paint inside.

It is just as well to remember that once the deck is on, it will be found difficult to paint the inside, and impossible to reach the bow and stern, so that now is the time to do the job. Use a good oil paint and give the woodwork and canvas at least two good coats, allowing each to dry before applying the next.

When the inside has dried, the surplus canvas at the gunwales can be trimmed off and turned under the gunwales as shown on the full-size drawing. In order to do this, you will find it necessary to cut the edges of the canvas where the frames are encountered.

Before the deck is put on it is advisable to fit the burden boards (or floor boards). These should be made in four sections for easy removal, the centre board only being fixed. This is screwed to the frames and extends from frame A to frame G. It will be found an advantage to be able to lift out these boards, because when the canoe has been in use for some time sand from the canoeists' feet, leaves, etc., will find their way into the bottom of the canoe and will have to be removed. Also, it will facilitate painting at the annual overhaul.

As explained already, the floor boards are screwed to a piece of $\frac{1}{2}$ in. square wood at each frame. This square member, fitting as it does against the frame, keeps the section in position. This is clearly shown in the drawings of the frames. When completed, the floor boards should be painted to match the rest of the interior, and put aside to dry while the deck is fitted.

The next job is the fitting of the cockpit coamings. Frame F will provide the coaming at the stern and frame D will act as a stretcher. Commence by fitting the $\frac{7}{8}$ in. square member to frame F fitting it into the notches already prepared in the frames. These will help to hold the square member in position while it is screwed to the frames. As the square members are carried forward they will bend and finally meet on frame B.

When these two members have been fixed, commence fitting the coamings proper, and don't forget to start at the stern. It is advisable to screw the coamings temporarily to

C

the squares and while they are held in this position to cut them to length. Take care to make a neat joint at the forward end of the cockpit. Having fitted them, they must now be removed as they cannot be finally fixed until the canvas deck is in position.

The fore deck centre rib and the carlines are the next items to be fixed and when this has been done all is ready to receive the canvas deck.

You fit the stern deck first, and this extends from the stern to the stern coaming, at frame F. Commence by tacking the canvas to the ⅞ in. square which has already been fixed to the rear of the stern coaming. The usual coat of white lead having been first applied, stretch the canvas to the stern. Stretch it over both gunwales, using tacks to hold it in position while the surplus material is cut off. One inch at least should be allowed all round the outside of the canoe.

A coat of white lead is now applied to the side of the gunwale to form a bed for the edge of the deck canvas which comes over ¼ in. and is turned under itself ½ in. so that no raw edge is left showing. The canvas should now be tacked to the gunwale at 1 in. intervals. The line of tacks will later be covered by a rubbing strip.

The two side decks are treated in a similar manner, the canvas being first tacked to the ⅞ in. cockpit member, then strained over the gunwale, tacked, the after end being turned under on Frame F, and tacked to the frame. The two forward ends are taken over frame B and will in turn be covered by the turned-under after end of the foredeck. The same procedure is followed at the gunwales as with the stern deck.

The foredeck canvas is stretched from the fore end of the cockpit to the bow, the after end being fixed as before, and the gunwales in a like manner.

Wherever a joint occurs it is essential that white lead should be applied to ensure a watertight joint, and all raw edges should be turned under.

The cockpit coamings can now be replaced and screwed to the ⅞ in. pieces. The rubbing strips can then be fixed to the gunwales, and the whole canoe given a coat of paint containing plenty of linseed oil. When dry, two further coats of good quality oil paint should be applied in order to finish the job off properly.

In painting it is important to apply thinly and evenly, and each coat must be allowed to dry thoroughly before the next is applied. Never forget that the paint is the protective covering as well as the waterproofing medium, and it is essential that nothing but the best quality paint be used. The extra expense involved will be cheaper in the long run.

Regarding colour, this is largely a matter for individual taste, but you might bear in mind that bright colours withstand the harmful action of the sun's rays better than dark ones. Aluminium, bright red, and white are better than dark blue, grey or green.

If a really first-class job is required, there are on the market various makes of rubberised paints that are specially recommended. They are impervious to sun, salt or oil, and while they are more expensive than oil or lead paints they are well worth it. They do not crack or blister, they are harder, and two coats are usually sufficient. Also, they are lighter in weight and give a lasting finish. If a glossy finish is desired, a coat of yatch, or superfine boat varnish can be added, but under no circumstances must rubberised paint be used on top of oil paint, as the latter will have a harmful effect upon it. Lastly, follow the manufacturers' instructions.

All that is required now to make the canoe ready for launching is two lengths of ½ in. half-round iron to be shaped to the bow and stern and fixed by screws. The top is bent round in the form of a half circle and fixed to the deck. The bottom follows the curve at the bottom of bow and stern and protects these when grounding. The loops at the top wilɪ be used for attaching the painters.

All that remains to complete the instructions is to supply a schedule of quantities, which will be found on pages 20-21.

The wood recommended is Oregon pine or red deal throughout, or if a better job is desired ash should be used for the frames and the cockpit coamings, oak for the keel, stem and stern, and all other members of Oregon pine. If ash is used for the frames, the thickness could be reduced to $\frac{3}{8}$ in. thick.

All the dimensions given are of finished sizes, and this should be made quite clear when ordering timber, as it is the custom of timber merchants to supply sizes rough sawn without allowance for planing unless specified.

TWO-SEATER HARD CHINE KAYAK.
SCHEDULE OF QUANTITIES.

Part	Size	Length	Quantity	Length	Size No.
	TIMBER		SCREWS		
Frame A	2″ × ½″	3′ 6″	12	1″	10
	3½″ × ½″	8″			
Frame B	2″ × ½″	6′ 3″	16	1″	10
Frame C	2″ × ½″	6′ 0″	12	1″	10
Frame D	2″ × ½″	8′ 9″	12	1″	10
	3½″ × ½″	1′ 7″	2	2″	8
			2	1″	8
Frame E	2″ × ½″	6′ 3″	12	1″	10
Frame F	3½″ × ½″	1′ 4″	2	2″	8
	2″ × ½″	6′ 8″	12	1″	10
Frame G	2″ × ½″	3′ 9″	6	1″	10
Stem	2″ × 2″	1′ 0″			
Stern	2″ × 2″	9″			
False Bow	⅞″ × ⅞″	1′ 0″	6	2″	8
			12	1″	8
			1	1½″	8
False Stern	⅞″ × ⅞″	9″			
Knees	3½″ × ½″	1′ 0″	5	2″	8
			2	2½″	8
			1	3″	8

SCHEDULE OF QUANTITIES—*continued.*

Part	Size	Length	Quantity	Length	Size No.
	TIMBER		SCREWS		
Breasthooks	$3\frac{1}{2}'' \times \frac{1}{2}''$	$9''$	8	$1\frac{1}{4}''$	8
Keel	$2'' \times 1''$	$18'\,0''$	9	$2''$	8
False Keel	$1'' \times 1''$	$16'\,0''$	12	$2''$	8
Gunwales, Two	$\frac{7}{8}'' \times \frac{7}{8}''$	$17'\,0''$	14	$2''$	8
			4	$1\frac{1}{4}''$	8
Chines, Two	$\frac{7}{8}'' \times \frac{7}{8}''$	$17'\,0''$	14	$2''$	8
			4	$1\frac{1}{4}''$	8
Stringers, Four	$\frac{3}{4}'' \times \frac{3}{8}''$	$11'\,3''$	24	$1\frac{1}{2}''$	8
Rubbing Strips, Six	$\frac{3}{4}'' \times \frac{1}{4}''$	$11'\,0''$	36	$\frac{7}{8}''$	8
Carlines, Two	$\frac{3}{4}'' \times \frac{1}{2}''$	$8'\,9''$	10	$1''$	8
Cockpit, Two	$\frac{7}{8}'' \times \frac{7}{8}''$	$11'\,3''$	12	$1\frac{1}{2}''$	8
Two	$3\frac{1}{2}'' \times \frac{3}{8}''$	$8'\,9''$	36	$1\frac{1}{4}''$	8
Fore deck Rib	$\frac{3}{4}'' \times \frac{3}{4}''$	$3'\,6''$	3	$2''$	8
Gunwale Rubbing Strip Two	$\frac{1}{2}''$ half round	$17'\,0''$			
	$\frac{1}{2}''$ half round	$3'\,6''$	76	$1''$	6 raised heads
Burden Boards	$3'' \times \frac{3}{8}''$	$13'\,0''$	66	$1''$	8
Two	$3'' \times \frac{3}{8}''$	$11'\,0''$			
Two	$3'' \times \frac{3}{8}''$	$8'\,6''$			
Burden Board Strips	$\frac{1}{2}'' \times \frac{1}{2}''$	$7'\,0''$	36	$\frac{7}{8}''$	8

TOTAL QUANTITY OF MATERIALS REQUIRED.

TIMBER			SCREWS	
$2' \times 1''$	$16'$	$0''$		
$2'' \times \frac{1}{2}''$	$41'$	$3''$	1	No. 8 × 3″ Countersunk heads
$1'' \times 1''$	$16'$	$0''$	82	No. 10 × 1″ ,, ,,
$\frac{7}{8}'' \times \frac{7}{8}''$	$92'$	$3''$	76	No. 6 × 1″ raised heads
$3\frac{1}{2}'' \times \frac{1}{2}''$	$5'$	$4''$	2	No. 8 × 2½″ Countersunk heads
$\frac{1}{2}'' \times \frac{1}{2}''$	$7'$	$0''$	66	No. 8 × 2″ Countersunk heads
$3'' \times \frac{3}{8}''$	$52'$	$0''$	90	No. 8 × 1″ ,, ,,
$\frac{1}{2}''$ half round	$37'$	$6''$		
$\frac{3}{4}'' \times \frac{3}{4}''$	$3'$	$6''$	37	No. 8 × 1½″ ,, ,,
$\frac{3}{4}'' \times \frac{1}{4}''$	$83'$	$6''$	52	No. 8 × 1¼″ ,, ,,
$\frac{3}{4}'' \times \frac{3}{8}''$	$45'$	$9''$	72	No. 8 × $\frac{7}{8}''$,, ,,
$2'' \times 2''$	$1'$	$9''$		Allow a few extra of each for making
$3\frac{1}{2}'' \times \frac{3}{8}''$	$17'$	$6''$		good damage or loss.

CANVAS.—10 yards, 48″ wide.
COPPER TACKS.—2 lbs., $\frac{5}{8}''$.
IRON.—$\frac{1}{2}''$ half round iron, 4′ 0″.

No. 1.—The first stage. Frames held in position on the building plank with angle brackets.

No. 2.—Lining the frames up on the building plank.

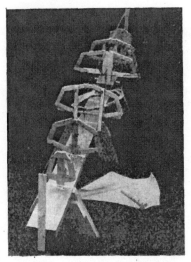

No. 3. —The assembly of the frames on the building plank.

No. 4.—Showing the method of assembling the bow and stern pieces.

No. 5.—The framework nears completion.

No. 6.—The nearly completed framework from another angle.

No. 7.—Fixing the false keel.

No. 8.—Showing the flair of the bow, specially designed to cause it to lift and not to wallow.

No. 9.—Showing inside of bow after hull canvas has been fixed, now ready for deck canvas.

No. 10.—The canvas fixed.   Craft now ready for deck canvas.

No. 11.—The completed craft, bottom upwards.

By

R. O. BUCK

WITH its low ends and flat bottom, which extends well up into bow and stern, this 16-ft., Canadian-type canoe is well adapted to the needs of the average builder. It is used by the forestry service because of its steadiness on the water, ease of paddling and the fact that it is little affected by cross winds on account of its wide beam which is 33 in. amidships. The weight of the finished canoe will be about 70 or 80 pounds.

Construction begins with a temporary framework consisting of a set of molds and a backbone, to which the molds are fastened. Paper patterns are made from the squared drawings, Figs. 1 and 2, to trace the outline of the molds on the stock. Each mold is made in two halves, fastened together temporarily with cleats. As both ends of the canoe are identical, two molds of each size, with the exception of the cen-

ter one, are required. The backbone is a piece of ¾-in. stock 5¼ in. wide and 14 ft. 6 in. long on the upper edge and 14 ft. 4½ in. on the lower edge. See Figs. 3 and 7. The keelson is a piece of clear, straight-grained ash or oak, cut to size and tapered at each end as shown in Fig. 7.

Bending canoe stems is a cranky job, even with special equipment for the business, so you use stems built up from regular stock as in Fig. 6. The grain should run nearly at right angles as in Fig. 7, and casein glue and dowels should be used in the joint.

Assembly is started by locating and nailing the molds in position along the backbone, as in Figs. 3 and 7. The frame is then turned over and the keelson nailed temporarily to each of the molds, after which the stem pieces are screwed between the cleats at the ends of the backbone, Fig. 7.

Own CANOE

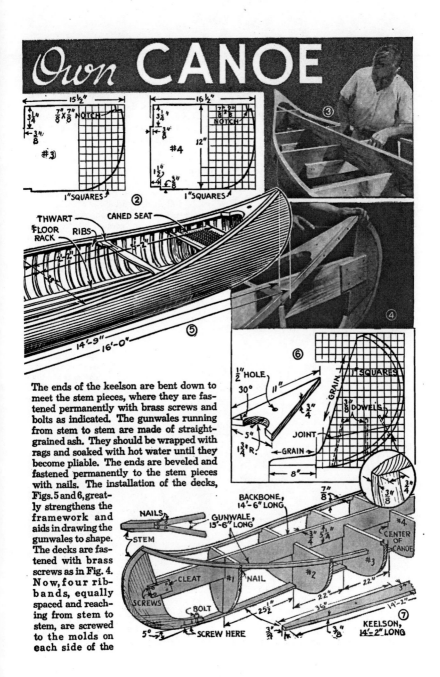

The ends of the keelson are bent down to meet the stem pieces, where they are fastened permanently with brass screws and bolts as indicated. The gunwales running from stem to stem are made of straight-grained ash. They should be wrapped with rags and soaked with hot water until they become pliable. The ends are beveled and fastened permanently to the stem pieces with nails. The installation of the decks, Figs. 5 and 6, greatly strengthens the framework and aids in drawing the gunwales to shape. The decks are fastened with brass screws as in Fig. 4. Now, four ribbands, equally spaced and reaching from stem to stem, are screwed to the molds on each side of the

57

saw is equipped with a ripping fence you will be able to save money on the ribs and planking by resawing them yourself, as shown in Fig. 10. The planks are soaked for several hours, then the first full-length plank is laid with the edge parallel with the center line of the keelson, Fig. 11, using clamps to draw it into place. Copper nails are used for fastening the planking to the ribs and all nails must be clinched across the grain on the inside of the ribs, Fig. 12. Fig. 11 shows the arrangement of the planking. Notice that the first five bilge planks run from stem to stem on each side of the keelson. The freeboard planks run out to points fore and aft as shown.

To remove the backbone, take out the cleats and saw it through at the center. Take out all but the No. 3 molds. Bolt the maple thwarts, Figs. 5 and 16, to the underside of the gunwales to prevent the hull from springing out of shape. The seat frames, Figs. 5 and 18, also may be fitted at this time. Actual measurement must determine the length of the seat stretchers. The rear stretchers are bolted direct to the

keelson as shown in Figs. 8 and 9.

Although the 2-in. white-cedar ribs are ³⁄₁₆ in. thick instead of the usual ¼ or ⁵⁄₁₆ in., this variation does not weaken the construction as the ribs are spaced 1 in. apart to compensate. Steaming, Fig. 13, is necessary to make them sufficiently pliable to take the bends. Each rib should be long enough to reach from gunwale to gunwale over the outside of the ribbands. Begin at the center and install each rib as shown in Fig. 14, drawing it into position with C-clamps and nailing at the keelson and gunwales, starting at the center of the canoe and working toward the ends. The ribs in front of the first mold are bent so sharply that it is practically impossible to prevent them from splintering. Where a rib comes over a mold, it is simply spaced out and omitted temporarily, Fig. 15, until the molds have been removed.

When the ribs are all in place, the ribbands are taken off, making the job ready for the ⅛-in. cedar planking. If your band

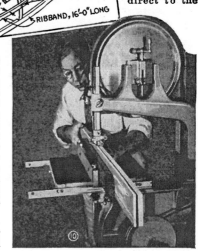

gunwales but the two forward are lowered 3 in. by means of hardwood spacers as in Fig. 18.

For canvassing you need two pieces of 8-oz. canvas, long enough to reach from stem to stem with about a foot to spare, and wide enough to reach from the gunwale to the keel with allowance for a lap. Start by spreading the canvas over half of the canoe, tacking temporarily near the center of the gunwale. Pull the covering tightly around the bilge and place a few tacks along the keel, near the center. Wet the canvas and pull it lengthwise over the stems, and tack. As it dries, the fabric will stretch and take the shape of the hull. When dry, pull out the tacks at one end and fit the canvas neatly around the stem,

PLANKS #1, 2, 3 AND 4—3" WIDE
PLANKING, 1" WHITE CEDAR
PLANK #5—2" WIDE
KEELSON
NAILS ARE CLINCHED ACROSS THE GRAIN
C-CLAMPS
RIBBANDS
TRIM OFF NAIL HERE
RIB

from the point of the keel to the gunwale, lapping 1 in. over the stem. Fasten with ¾-in. copper tacks, spaced 1 in. apart. Then remove all other temporary tacks and roll the canvas back off the canoe.

Beginning at the tacked end, apply a coat of waterproof canvas cement to a section of the planking along the keel, using a stiff brush, Fig. 17. Do not cover a large area as the cement dries quickly. Unroll the canvas over the cemented area, pull tightly lengthwise and fasten the loose end temporarily while tacks are placed closely along the gunwale and keel of the cemented portion. As you tack be sure that the cloth lies flat without any wrinkles. Then squeegee the canvas with the palm of the hand to make sure that it is in contact with the cement at all points. Take the next section of the hull in the same manner continuing by successive stages until you finish at the opposite stem. The second half is stretched and tacked in the same manner as the first allowing for the lap under the keel. This done, you trim the canvas along

59

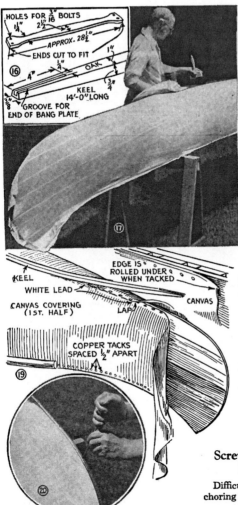

and varnished. Apply the gunwale molding, Fig. 19, with roundhead brass nails, and finish the canoe inside and out with two coats of spar varnish. In varnishing the inside, care should be taken to prevent the varnish "piling up" in corners between the ribs and planking. Two thin coats are much more durable and less apt to check. Finally the keel is varnished separately and screwed in place as in Fig. 19. Finish up with the ¼-in. half-round copper bang plates.

Screws Held in Pressed Wood by Cellulose Cement

Difficulty of anchoring screws in pressed wood is overcome by filling the hole drilled to drive the screw with cellulose cement or thick lacquer. After it has dried the screw is driven into place. Within an hour the cement will have dried to the pressed wood about the screw so that the latter is held securely.

the gunwales and finish tacking the stems, using copper tacks, which should be spaced about ½ in. apart.

Allow a few days for drying, then apply a coat of canvas cement over the entire surface. When dry, sand smooth and finish with one coat of deck paint and one of flat color after which it is again sanded

60

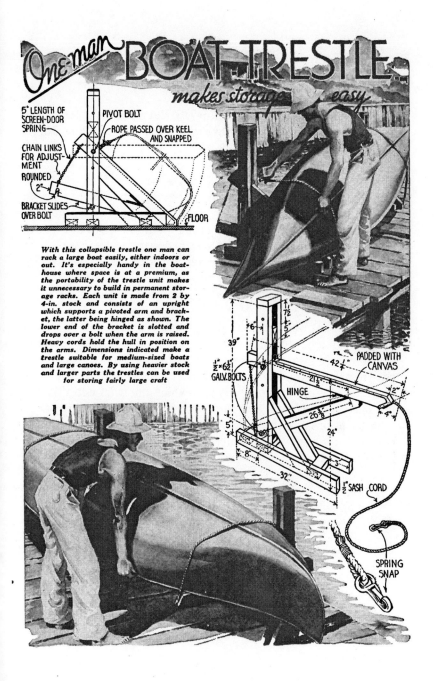

One-man BOAT-TRESTLE

makes storage easy

5" LENGTH OF SCREEN-DOOR SPRING

PIVOT BOLT

ROPE PASSED OVER KEEL AND SNAPPED

CHAIN LINKS FOR ADJUSTMENT

ROUNDED 2"

BRACKET SLIDES OVER BOLT

FLOOR

With this collapsible trestle one man can rack a large boat easily, either indoors or out. It's especially handy in the boathouse where space is at a premium, as the portability of the trestle unit makes it unnecessary to build in permanent storage racks. Each unit is made from 2 by 4-in. stock and consists of an upright which supports a pivoted arm and bracket, the latter being hinged as shown. The lower end of the bracket is slotted and drops over a bolt when the arm is raised. Heavy cords hold the hull in position on the arms. Dimensions indicated make a trestle suitable for medium-sized boats and large canoes. By using heavier stock and larger parts the trestles can be used for storing fairly large craft

7½"
6"
5"
39"
½"x6½" GALV. BOLTS
42¼"
PADDED WITH CANVAS
21½"
HINGE
2"
4"
26⅜"
24"
5"
8"
3"
32"
½" SASH CORD
SPRING SNAP

CANOES

The Advantages of a Canoe—How to Make the Slab Canoe and the Dugout—How to Make a Siwash and a White Man's Dugout

THERE are many small freak crafts invented each year, but none of them has any probabilities of being popularly used as substitutes for the old models.

Folding canoes, as a rule, are cranky, but the writer has found them most convenient when it was necessary to transport them long distances overland. They are not, however, the safest of crafts; necessarily they lack the buoyant wooden frame and lining of the ordinary canvas canoe, which enables it to float even when filled with water.

The author owes his life to the floating properties of his canvas canoe. On one occasion when it upset in a driving easterly storm the wind was off shore, and any attempt upon the canoeist's part to swim toward shore would have caused him to have been suffocated by the tops of the waves which the wind cut off, driving the water with stinging force into his face so constantly that, in order to breathe at all, he had to face the other way. He was at length rescued by a steamer, losing nothing but the sails and his shoes. Nevertheless, the same storm which capsized his little craft upset several larger boats and tore the sails from others.

The advantages of a good canoe are many for the young navigators: they can launch their own craft, pick it up when occasion demands and carry it overland. It is safe in experienced hands in any weather which is fit for out-door amusement. When you are "paddling your own canoe" you are facing to the front and can see what is ahead of you, which is much safer and more pleasant than travelling backward, like a crawfish.

The advance-guard of modern civilization is the lumberman, and following close on his heels comes the all-devouring saw-mill. This fierce creature has an abnormal appetite for logs,

THE SLAB

Fig. 40.

and it keeps an army of men, boys, and horses busy in supplying it with food. While it supplies us with lumber for the carpenter, builder, and cabinet-maker, it at the same time, in the most shameful way, fills the trout streams and rivers with great masses of sawdust, which kills and drives away the fish. But near the saw-mill there is always to be found material for a

Slab Canoe

which consists simply of one of those long slabs, the first cut from some giant log (Fig. 43).

These slabs are burned or thrown away by the mill-owners, and hence cost nothing; and as the saw-mill is in advance of population, you are most likely to run across one on a hunting or fishing trip.

Near one end, and on the flat side of the slab (Fig. 40), bore four holes, into which drive the four legs of a stool made of a section of a smaller slab (Fig. 41), and your boat is ready to launch. From a piece of board make a double or single paddle (Fig. 42), and you are equipped for a voyage. An old gentleman, who in his boyhood days on the frontier frequently used this simple style of canoe, says that the speed it makes will compare favor-

.

ably with that of many a more pretentious vessel. See Fig. 43 for furnished boat.

The Dugout

Although not quite as delicate in model or construction as the graceful birch-bark canoe, the "dugout" of the Indians is a

Fig. 41.

most wonderful piece of work, when we consider that it is carved from the solid trunk of a giant tree with the crudest of tools, and is the product of savage labor.

Few people now living have enjoyed the opportunity of seeing one built by the Indians, and, as the author is not numbered among that select few, he considers it a privilege to be able to quote the following interesting account given by Mr. J. H. Mallett, of Helena.

How to Build a Siwash Canoe

"While visiting one of the small towns along Puget Sound, I was greatly interested in the way the Indians built their canoes.

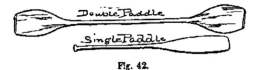

Fig. 42.

It is really wonderful how these aborigines can, with the crudest means and with a few days' work, convert an unwieldy log into a trim and pretty canoe.

"One Monday morning I saw a buck building a fire at the base of a large cedar-tree, and he told me that this was the first step in the construction of a canoe that he intended to use upon the following Saturday. He kept the fire burning merrily all that day and far into the night, when a wind came up and completed

Fig. 43.—Slab canoe.

the downfall of the monarch of the forest. The next day the man arose betimes, and, borrowing a cross-cut saw from a logger, cut the trunk of the tree in twain at a point some fifteen feet from where it had broken off, and then with a dull hatchet he hacked away until the log had assumed the shape of the desired canoe. In this work he was helped by his squaw. The old fellow then built a fire on the upper part of the log, guiding the course of the fire with daubs of clay, and in due course of time the interior of the canoe had been burned out. Half a day's work with the hatchet rendered the inside smooth and shapely.

"The canoe was now, I thought, complete, though it appeared to be dangerously narrow of beam. This the Indian soon remedied. He filled the shell two-thirds full of water, and into the fluid he dropped half a dozen stones that had been heating in the fire for nearly a day. The water at once attained a boiling point, and so softened the wood that the buck and squaw were enabled to draw out the sides and thus supply the necessary breadth of beam. Thwarts and slats were then placed in the canoe and the water and stones thrown out. When the steamed wood began to cool and contract, the thwarts held it

Fig. 44.—The dugout.

back, and the sides held the thwarts, and there the canoe was complete, without a nail, joint, or crevice, for it was made of one piece of wood. The Siwash did not complete it as soon as he had promised, but it only took him eight days."

In the North-eastern part of our country, before the advent of the canvas canoe, beautiful and light birch-bark craft were used by the Indians, the voyagers, trappers, and white woodsmen. But in the South and in the North-west, the dugout takes the place of the birch-bark. Among the North-western Indians the dugouts are made from the trunks of immense cedar-trees and built with high, ornamental bows, which are brilliantly decorated with paint. On the eastern shore of Maryland and Virginia the dugout is made into a sail-boat called the buck-eye,

Boat-Building and Boating

or bug-eye. But all through the Southern States, from the Ohio River to the Gulf of Mexico and in Mexico, the dugout is made of a hollowed log after the manner of an ordinary horse trough, and often it is as crude as the latter, but it can be made almost as beautiful and graceful as a birch-bark canoe.

How to Make a White Man's Dugout Canoe

To make one of these dugout canoes one must be big and strong enough to wield an axe, but if the readers are too young

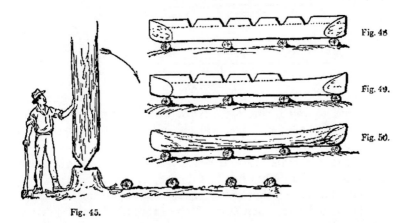

Fig. 48

Fig. 49.

Fig. 50.

Fig. 45.

for this work, they are none too young to know how to make one, and their big brothers and father can do the work. Since the dugout occupies an important position in the history of our country, every boy scout should know how it is made.

Fig. 44 shows one of these canoes afloat; Fig. 45 shows a tall, straight tree suitable for our purpose, and it also shows how the tree is cut and the arrangement of the kerfs, or two notches, so that it will fall in the direction of the arrow in the diagram. You will notice along the ground are shown the ends of a number of small logs. These are the skids, or rollers, upon which the log will rest when the tree is cut and felled. The tree will fall in the direction

Canoes

in which the arrow is pointed if there is no wind. If you have never cut down a tree, be careful to take some lessons of a good woodsman before you attempt it.

When the log is trimmed off at both ends like Fig. 46, flatten the upper side with the axe. This is for the bottom of the canoe; the flat part should be about a foot and a half wide to extend

Fig. 46.

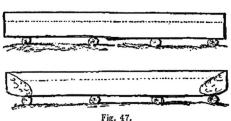

Fig. 47.

from end to end of the log. Now, with some poles for pryers, turn your log over so that it will rest with the flat bottom on the skids, as in Fig. 46.

Next take a chalk-line and fasten it at the two ends of the log, as shown by the dotted line in Figs. 46, 47, 48, 49.

Snap the line so that it will make a straight mark as shown by the dotted line; then trim off the two ends for the bow and stern, as shown in Fig. 47. Next cut notches down to the dotted line, as illustrated in Fig. 48; then cut away from the bow down to the first notch, making a curved line, as shown in Fig. 49 (which is cut to second notch). Do the same with the stern, making duplicates of the bow and stern. The spaces between the notches amidships may now be split off by striking your axe along the chalk-line and then carefully driving in wooden wedges. When this is all done you will have Fig. 50. You can now turn the log over and trim off the edges of the bow and stern so that they will slope, as shown in Fig. 44, in a rounded curve; after which roll the canoe back again upon its bottom and with an adze and axe hollow out the inside, leaving some solid wood at both bow

68

and stern—not that you need the wood for strength, but to save labor. When you have decided upon the thickness of the sides of your canoe, take some small, pointed instrument, like an awl, for instance, and make holes with it to the required depth at intervals along the sides and bottom of the canoe. Then take some small sticks (as long as the canoe sides are to be thick), make them to fit the holes, blacken their ends, and drive them into the holes.

As soon as you see one from the inside, you will know that you have made the shell thin enough. Use a jack-plane to smooth it off inside and out; then build a big fire and heat some stones. Next fill the canoe with water and keep dumping the hot stones in the water until the latter is almost or quite to boiling point. The hot water will soften the wood so that the sides will become flexible, and you can then fit in some braces at the bow, stern, and centre of the canoe. Make the centre brace or seat some inches wider than the log, so that when it is forced in place it will spread the canoe in the middle.

CANOES AND BOATING STUNTS

**How to Build a War Canoe—How to Build a Canvas Canoe—
How to Build an Umbrella Canoe—How Old Shells Can be
Turned into Boys' Boats—Cause of Upsets—Landing from,
and Embarking in, a Shell—How to Mend Checks and Cracks**

In making canoes the Indians used birch bark for the cover, rock maple for the cross-bars, and white cedar for the rest of the frame. We will substitute canvas for the birch bark and any old wood that we can for the rock maple and the white cedar. *Real woodcraft is best displayed in the ability to use the material at hand.*

David Abercrombie, the outfitter, some time ago presented Andrew J. Stone, the Arctic explorer and mighty hunter, with a small piece of light, water-proof cloth to use as a shelter tent in bad weather. But Stone, like the hunter that he was, slept unprotected on the mountain side in the sleet and driving storms, and used the water-proof cloth to protect the rare specimens he had shot. One day a large, rapid torrent lay in his path; there was no lumber large enough with which to build a raft, and the only wood for miles around was small willow bushes growing along the river bank. At his command, his three Indians made a canoe frame of willow sticks, tied together with bits of cloth and string. Stone set this frame in the middle of his water-proof cloth, tied the cloth over the frame with other pieces of string, and using only small clubs for paddles, he and his men crossed the raging torrent in this makeshift, which was loaded with their guns, camera, and specimens that he had shot on the trip.

Boat-Building and Boating

After reading the above there is no doubt the reader will be able to build a war canoe with barrel-hoop ribs and lattice-work slats. In the writer's studio is a long piece of maple, one and one-half inches wide and one-quarter inch thick, which was left by the workmen when they put down a hard-wood floor. If you can get some similar strips, either of oak, maple, or birch, from the dealers in flooring material, they will not be expensive and will make splendid gunwales for your proposed canoe. There should be four such strips. The hard-wood used for flooring splits easily, and holes should be bored for the nails or screws to prevent cracking the wood when the nails or screws are driven home. Fig. 51 shows the framework (side view) of the canoe; Fig. 52 shows an end view of the same canoe; Fig. 53 shows the middle section, and Fig. 54 shows the form of the bow and stern sections. This boat may be built any length you wish, and so that you may get the proper proportions, the diagrams from one to five are marked off in equal divisions. To make patterns of the moulds, Figs. 53 and 54, take a large piece of manila paper, divide it up into the same number of squares as the diagram, make the squares any size you may decide upon, and then trace the line, 1–H–10, as it is in the diagrams. This will give you the patterns of the two moulds (Figs. 53 and 54). While you are looking at these figures, it may be well to call your attention to the way bow and stern pieces are made. In Fig. 63 the pieces Y and X are made from pieces of a packing-box, notched and nailed together with a top piece, U, and a brace, V.

The other end of the same canoe is, as you may see, strengthened and protected by having a barrel-hoop tacked over the stem-pieces, Y, X, U. In Fig. 64 we use different material; here the stem-piece is made of a broken bicycle rim, U, braced by the pieces of packing-box, Y, V, and W. The left-hand end of Fig. 64 is made with pieces of head of a barrel, X and U. The bottom of the stem-piece Y is made of the piece of a packingbox. The two braces V are parts of the barrel-stave. Fig. 60 shows the common form of the bow of a canoe. The stem-pieces

71

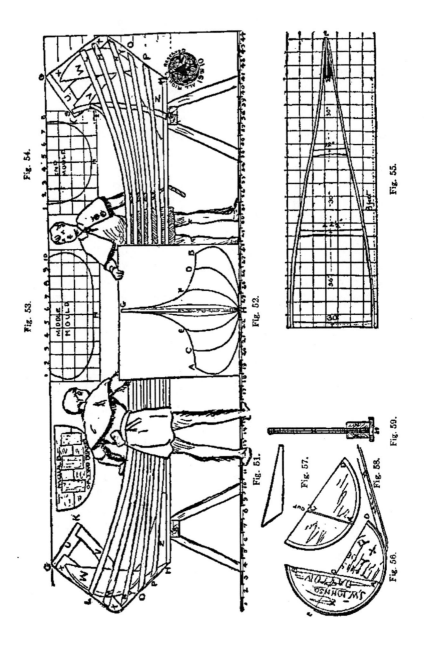

Fig. 53.

Fig. 54.

Fig. 55.

Fig. 52.

Fig. 56.

Fig. 57.

Fig. 58.

Fig. 59.

Fig. 51.

X, Y are made of the parts of the head of a barrel, as shown in
Fig. 62. To make a stem from a barrel-head, nail the two
pieces X and Y, Fig. 56, together as shown in this particular
diagram. Now take another piece of barrel-head, Fig. 57, and
saw off a piece, A', D', C', so that it will fit neatly over A, C, D,
on Fig. 56. Nail this securely in place, and then in the same
manner cut another piece to fit over the part E, C, B, and nail
that in place. Use small nails, but let them be long enough so
that you may clinch them by holding an axe or an iron against the
head while you hammer the protruding points down, or drive the
nail a little on the bias and holding the axe or iron on the side it is
to come through and let it strike the nail as it comes out and it
will clinch itself. To fasten the stem-piece to the keel use two
pieces of packing-box or board, cut in the form of Fig. 58, and
nail these securely to the bow-piece as in Z, in Fig. 60. Then
from the bottom side of the keel H, nail the keel-pieces firmly to
the keel as in Fig. 61. Also drive some nails from Z to the top
down to the keel, as shown by the dotted lines in Fig. 60. The
end view, Fig. 59, shows how the two Z pieces hug and support
the stem-piece on the keel H. Fig. 55 shows a half of the top
view of the canoe gunwales; the dimensions, marked in feet and
inches, are taken from an Indian birch-bark canoe. You see
by the diagram that it is eight feet from the centre of the middle
cross-piece to the end of the big opening at the bow. It is also
three feet from the centre of the middle cross-piece to the next
cross-piece, and thirty inches from the centre of that cross-piece
to the bow cross-piece, which is just thirty inches from the eight-
foot mark. The middle cross-piece in a canoe of these dimensions is seven-eighths of an inch thick, and thirty inches long between the gunwales; the next cross-piece is three-quarters of an
inch thick and twenty-two and one-half inches long. The next
one is half an inch wide, two inches thick and twelve inches between the gunwales. These cross-pieces can be made of the
staves of a barrel. Of course, this would be a canoe of sixteen
feet inside measurement, not counting the flattened part of the

bow and stern. Now, then, to build the canoe. First take the keel-piece, H, which is in this case a piece of board about six inches wide and only thick enough to be moderately stiff. Lay the keel on any level surface and put the stem-pieces on as already described, using packing-box for X, U, V, Y, and Z, and

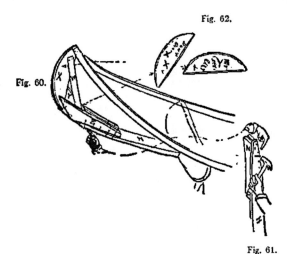

Fig. 62.

Fig. 60.

Fig. 61.

Conventional bow, but made of barrel-heads.

bracing them with a piece of packing-box on each side, marked W in diagram (Fig. 51). Then make three moulds, one for the centre (Fig. 53), and two more for the bow and stern (Fig. 54). Notch the bottom of these moulds to fit the keel and with wire nails make them fast to the keel, leaving the ends of the nails protruding far enough to be easily withdrawn when you wish to remove the moulds. In nailing the laths to the moulds (Fig. 51) leave the heads of the nails also protruding so that they may be removed. Place the moulds in position, with the middle one in the exact centre, and the two ends located like those in Figs. 63 and 64. Place and nail gunwale, L, on as in Fig. 51, tacking it to the bow and stern and bending it around to fit the moulds;

tack the lattice slats M, N, O, P on to the bow, stern, and moulds, as shown in Fig. 51.

If your barrel-hoops are stiff and liable to break while bending and unbending, let them soak a couple of days in a tub of water, then before fitting them to the form of the canoe make them more pliable by pouring hot water on them. The barrel-hoop S, R, at the bow of the canoe, is nailed to the top-piece U, to the inside of the slats L, M, N, O, P, and to the outside of H. The next three ribs on each side are treated in the same manner; repeat this at the other end of the canoe and nail the intervening ribs to the top of H and to the inside of the slats, following the model of the boat. Put the ribs about four inches apart and clinch the nails as already described.

In the diagrams there is no temporary support for the canoe frame except the wooden horses, as in Fig. 51. These supports have been purposely omitted in the drawing, as it is desirable to keep it as simple as possible. Some temporary support will be necessary to hold the bow and stern-piece in Fig. 51. These supports can be nailed or screwed temporarily to the canoe frame so as to hold it rigid while you are at work on it.

After the ribs are all in place and the framework completed, turn the canoe upside down upon the wooden horses—for a canoe as large as the one in the first diagram you will need three horses, one at each end and one in the middle. For a canoe of the dimensions marked in Fig. 55, that is, sixteen feet inside measurement, you would need about seven yards of ten-ounce cotton canvas, of sufficient width to reach up over the sides of your canoe. Take a tape-measure or a piece of ordinary tape or a long strip of manila paper and measure around the bottom of the boat at its widest part in the middle from one gunwale (top of side) to the other, and see that your cloth is fully as wide as your measurement. Fold the canvas lengthwise so as to find its exact centre and crease it. With two or three tacks fasten the cloth at its centre line (the crease) to the stem-piece of the canoe. Stretch the canvas the length of the boat with the crease of centre-line along the centre of the keel, pull it as taut as may be and again tack the centre line to the stem at this end of the craft. If this has been done carefully the cloth will hang an equal length over each side of the canoe. Now begin amidships and drive tacks about two inches apart along the gunwale, say an inch below the top surface. After having tacked it for about two feet, go to the other side of

Fig. 63.

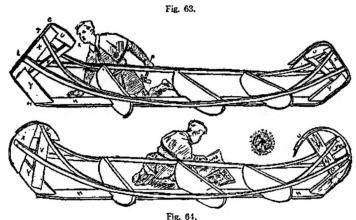

Fig. 64.
High bows framework made of packing-box and barrel-heads.

the boat, pull the cloth taut and in the same manner tack about three feet. Continue this process first one side and then the other until finished. While stretching the cloth knead it with the hand and fingers so as to thicken or "full" it where it would otherwise wrinkle; by doing this carefully it is possible to stretch the canvas over the frame without the necessity of cutting it. The cloth that extends beyond the frame may be brought over the gunwale and tacked along the inside. Use four-ounce tinned or copper tacks. The canvas is now stretched on every part except on the high, rolling bow and stern. With a pair of shears slit the canvas from the outer edge of the bow and stern within a half inch of the ends of the keel.

Fold the right-hand flap thus made at the left-hand end around the bow and stern and, drawing tight, tack it down, then fold the left-hand flap over the right-hand side and tack it in a similar manner, trimming off the remaining cloth neatly. The five braces, three of which are shown in Fig. 55, may be nailed to the gunwales of the canoe, as the temporary moulds are removed. The braces should be so notched that the top ends of the braces will fit over the top edge of the gunwale and their lower edges will fit against the sides. Give the boat at least three good coats of paint and nail the two extra gunwale strips on the outside of the canvas for guards.

When it is dry and the boat is launched you may startle the onlookers and make the echoes ring with:

"Wo-ach! wo-ach! Ha-ha-ha-hack—wo-ach!" which is said to be the identical war cry with which the Indians greeted the landing of our Pilgrim Fathers.

The reader must not suppose that barrel-hoops are the best material for ribs; they are but a makeshift, and although good-looking, servicable canoes have been built of this material from the foregoing descriptions, better ones may be made by using better material, such, for instance, as is described in the making of the birch-bark canoe.

Old Shells

Where there are oarsmen and boat-clubs, there you will find beautiful shell boats of paper or cedar, shaped like darning-needles, so slight in structure that a child can knock a hole in them, and yet very seaworthy boats for those who understand how to handle them. The expensive material and skilled labor necessary to build a racing shell puts the price of one so high that few boys can afford to buy one; but where new shells are to be found there are also old ones, and when they are too old to sell they are thrown away. Many an old shell rots on the meadows near the boat-houses or rests among the rafters forgotten and unused, which with a little work would make a boat capable of furnishing no end of fun to a boy.

Canoes and Boating Stunts

Checks or Cracks

can be pasted over with common manila wrapping-paper by
first covering the crack with a coat of paint, or, better still, of
varnish, then fitting the paper smoothly over the spot and varnishing the paper. Give the paper several coats of varnish, allowing it to dry after each application, and the paper will become
impervious to water. The deck of a shell is made of thin muslin
or paper, treated with a liberal coat of varnish, and can be patched
with similar material. There are always plenty of slightly damaged oars which have been discarded by the oarsmen. The use
of a saw and jack-knife in the hands of a smart boy can trans-
form these wrecks into serviceable oars for his patched-up old
shell, and if the work is neatly done, the boy will be the proud
owner of a real shell boat, and the envy of his comrades.

The Cause of Upsets

A single shell that is very cranky with a man in it is comparatively steady when a small boy occupies the seat. Put on your
bathing clothes when you wish to try a shell, so that you may be
ready for the inevitable upset. Every one knows, when he looks
at one of these long, narrow boats, that as long as the oars are
held extended *on the water* it cannot upset. But, in spite of that
knowledge, every one, when he first gets into a shell, endeavors
to balance himself by *lifting the oars*, and, of course, goes over in
a jiffy.

The Delights of a Shell

It is an error to suppose that the frail-looking, needle-like
boat is only fit for racing purposes. For a day on the water, in
calm weather, there is, perhaps, nothing more enjoyable than a
single shell. The exertion required to send it on its way is so
slight, and the speed so great, that many miles can be covered
with small fatigue. Upon referring to the log-book of the Nereus
Club, where the distances are all taken from the United States

chart, the author finds that twenty and thirty miles are not un-common records for single-shell rows.

During the fifteen or sixteen seasons that the author has devoted his spare time to the sport he has often planned a heavy cruising shell, but owing to the expense of having such a boat built he has used the ordinary racing boat, and found it remarkably well adapted for such purposes. Often he has been caught miles away from home in a blow, and only once does he remember of being compelled to seek assistance.

He was on a lee shore and the waves were so high that after once being swamped he was unable to launch his boat again, for it would fill before he could embark. So a heavy rowboat and a coachman were borrowed from a gentleman living on the bay, and while the author rowed, the coachman towed the little craft back to the creek where the Nereus club-house is situated.

In the creek, however, the water was calmer, and rather than stand the jeers of his comrades, the writer embarked in his shell and rowed up to the boat-house float. He was very wet and his boat was full of water, but to the inquiry of "Rough out in the bay?" he confined himself to the simple answer—"Yes." Then dumping the water from his shell and placing it upon the rack he put on his dry clothes and walked home, none the worse for the accident.

After ordinary skill and confidence are acquired it is really astonishing what feats can be accomplished in a frail racing boat.

It is not difficult to

Stand Upright In a Shell

if you first take one of your long stockings and tie the handles of your oars together where they cross each other in front of you. The ends will work slightly and the blades will keep their positions on the water, acting as two long balances. Now slide your seat as far forward as it will go, slip your feet from the straps and grasp the staps with your hand, moving the feet back to a comfortable position. When all ready raise yourself by pulling on the foot

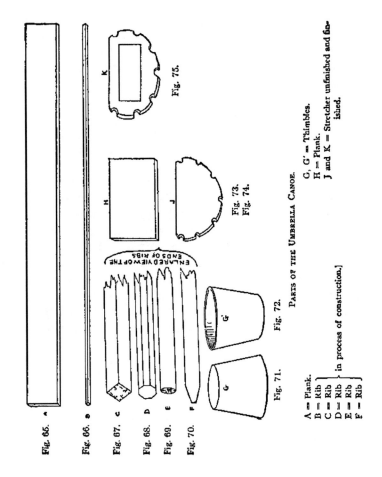

Fig. 65.

Fig. 66.

Fig. 67.

Fig. 68.

Fig. 69.

Fig. 70.

Fig. 71.

Fig. 72.

Fig. 73.
Fig. 74.

Fig. 75.

ENLARGED VIEW OF THE
ENDS OF RIBS

PARTS OF THE UMBRELLA CANOE.

A = Plank.
B = Rib
C = Rib
D = Rib } in process of construction.]
E = Rib
F = Rib

G, G' = Thimbles.
H = Plank.
J and K = Stretcher unfinished and fin-
ished.

Boat-Building and Boating

strap, and with ordinary care you can stand upright in the needle-shaped boat, an apparently impossible thing to do when you look at the narrow craft.

How to Land Where There Is No Float

When for any reason you wish to land where there is no float, row into shallow water and put one foot overboard until it touches bottom. Then follow with the other foot, rise, and you are standing astride of your boat.

How to Embark Where There Is No Float

Wade out and slide the shell between your extended legs until the seat is underneath you. Sit down, and, with the feet still in the water, grasp your oars. With these in your hands it is an easy task to balance the boat until you can lift your feet into it.

Ozias Dodge's Umbrella Canoe

Mr. Dodge is a Yale man, an artist, and an enthusiastic canoeist. The prow of his little craft has ploughed its way through the waters of many picturesque streams in this country and Europe, by the river-side, under the walls of ruined castles, where the iron-clad warriors once built their camp-fires, and near pretty villages, where people dress as if they were at a fancy-dress ball.

When a young man like Mr. Dodge says that he has built a folding canoe that is not hard to construct, is inexpensive and practical, there can be little doubt that such a boat is not only what is claimed for it by its inventor, but that it is a novelty in its line, and such is undoubtedly the case with the umbrella canoe.

How the Canoe Was Built

The artist first secured a white-ash plank (A, Fig. 65), free from knots and blemishes of all kinds. The plank was one inch thick and about twelve feet long. At the mill he had this sawed into eight strips one inch wide, one inch thick, and twelve feet long (B and C, Figs. 66 and 67). Then he planed off the square edges of each stick until they were all octagonal in form, and looked like so many great lead-pencils (D, Fig. 68).

Mr. Dodge claims that, after you have reduced the ash poles to this octagonal form, it is an easy matter to whittle them with

Fig. 76.—Frame of umbrella canoe.

your pocket-knife or a draw-knife, and by taking off all the angles of the sticks make them cylindrical in form (E, Fig. 69); then smooth them off nicely with sand-paper, so that each pole has a smooth surface and is three-quarters of an inch in diameter.

After the poles were reduced to this state he whittled all the ends to the form of a truncated cone—that is, like a sharpened lead-pencil with the lead broken off (F, Fig. 70)—a blunt point. He next went to a tinsmith and had two sheet-iron cups made large enough to cover the eight pole-ends (G and G', Figs. 71 and 72). Each cup was six inches deep. After trying the cups, or thimbles, on the poles to see that they would fit, he made two moulds of oak. First he cut two pieces of oak plank two feet six

Fig. 77.—Umbrella canoe.

inches long by one foot six inches (H, Fig. 74), which he trimmed into the form shown by J, Fig. 75, making a notch to fit each of the round ribs, and to spread them as the ribs of an umbrella are spread. He made two other similar moulds for the bow and stern, each of which, of course, is smaller than the middle one. After spreading the ribs with the moulds, and bringing the ends together in the tin cups, he made holes in the bottom of the cups where the ends of the ribs came, and fastened the ribs to the cups with brass screws, fitted with leather washers, and run through the holes in the tin and screwed into the ends of the poles or ribs.

Fig. 78.—Canoe folded for transportation. Canoe in water in distance.

A square hole was then cut through each mould (K, Fig. 75), and the poles put in place, gathered together at the ends, and held in place by the tin thimbles. The square holes in the moulds allow several small, light floor planks to form a dry floor to the canoe.

The canvas costs about forty-five cents a yard, and five yards are all you need. The deck can be made of drilling, which comes about twenty-eight inches wide and costs about twenty cents a yard. Five yards of this will be plenty. Fit your canvas over the frame, stretch it tightly, and tack it securely to the two top ribs only. Fasten the deck on in the same manner.

When Mr. Dodge had the canoe covered and decked, with a square hole amidship to sit in, he put two good coats of paint on the canvas, allowed it to dry, and his boat was ready for use (Fig. 77). He quaintly says that "it looked like a starved dog, with all its ribs showing through the skin," just as the ribs of an umbrella show on top through the silk covering. But this does not in any way impede the progress of the boat through the water.

Where the moulds are the case is different, for the lines of the moulds cross the line of progress at right angles and must necessarily somewhat retard the boat. But even this is not perceptible. The worst feature about the moulds is that the canvas is very apt to be damaged there by contact with the shore, float, or whatever object it rubs against.

With ordinary care the umbrella canoe

Will Last for Years

and is a good boat for paddling on inland streams and small bodies of water; and when you are through with it for the night, all that is necessary is to remove the stretchers by springing the poles from the notches in the spreaders, roll up the canvas around the poles, put it on your shoulder, and carry it home or to camp, as shown in Fig. 78.

To put your canoe together again put in the moulds, fit the poles in their places, and the umbrella is raised, or, rather, the canoe is, if we can use such an expression in regard to a boat.

How to Build a Real Birch-Bark Canoe or a Canvas Canoe on a "Birch-Bark" Frame—How to Mend a Birch-Bark

ALTHOUGH the Indian was the first to build these simple little boats, some of his white brothers are quite as expert in the work. But the red man can outdo his white brother in navigating the craft. The only tools required in building a canoe are a knife and awl, a draw-shave and a hammer. An Indian can do all of his work with a knife.

Several years ago canvas began to be used extensively in canoe-building, instead of birch bark, and it will eventually entirely supersede birch, although nothing can be found that bends so gracefully. There are several canvas-canoe factories in Maine, and the canoes made of canvas have both the symmetry and the durability of the birches. They are also a trifle cheaper, but if the real thing and sentiment are wanted, one should never have anything but a bark craft.

If properly handled, a good canoe will safely hold four men. Canoes intended for deep water should have considerable depth. Those intended for shoal water, such as trout-fishers use, are made as flat as possible. Up to the time when canoeing was introduced the materials for building craft of this kind could be found all along the rivers. Big birch-trees grew in countless numbers, and clear, straight cedar was quite as plentiful within a few feet of the water's edge. Now one must go miles back into the dense forests for such materials, and even then seldom does it happen that two suitable trees are found within sight of one or the other. Cedar is more difficult of the two to find.

The Birch-Bark

The Tree

The tree is selected, first, for straightness; second, smoothness; third, freedom from knots or limbs; fourth, toughness of bark; fifth, small size of eyes; sixth, length (the last is not so important, as two trees can be put together), and, seventh, size (which is also not so important, as the sides can be pieced out).

Dimensions

The average length of canoe is about 19 feet over all, running, generally, from 18 to 22 feet for a boat to be used on inland waters, the sea-going canoes being larger, with relatively higher bows. The average width is about 30 inches inside, measured along the middle cross-bar; the greatest width inside is several inches below the middle cross-bar, and is several inches greater than the width measured along said cross-bar.

The measurements given below are those of a canoe 19 feet over all: 16 feet long inside, measured along the curve of the gunwale; 30 inches wide inside. The actual length inside is less than 16 feet, but the measurement along the gunwales is the most important.

Bark

Bark can be peeled when the sap is flowing or when the tree is not frozen—at any time in late spring, summer, and early fall (called summer bark); in winter during a thaw, when the tree is not frozen, and when the sap may have begun to flow.

Difference in the Bark

Summer bark peels readily, is smooth inside, of a yellow color, which turns reddish upon exposure to the sun, and is chalky-gray in very old canoes. Winter bark adheres closely, and forcibly brings up part of the inner bark, which on exposure turns dark red. This rough surface may be moistened and scraped away. All winter-bark canoes must be thus scraped and made smooth. Sometimes the dark red is left in the form of a decorative pattern extending around the upper edge of the canoe, the rest of the surface being scraped smooth.

Process of Peeling

. The tree should be cut down so that the bark can be removed more easily.

A log called a skid (Fig. 79) is laid on the ground a few feet from the base of the tree, which will keep the butt of the tree off the ground when the tree is felled. The limbs at the top will

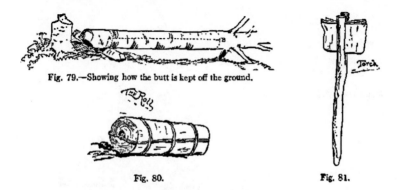

Fig. 79.—Showing how the butt is kept off the ground.

Fig. 80.

Fig. 81.

keep the other end off the ground. A space is cleared of bushes and obstructions where the tree is to fall.

After the tree has been cut down, a cut is made in a straight line (A, B, Fig. 79), splitting the bark from top to bottom, and a ring cut at A and B (Fig. 79). When sap is flowing, the bark is readily removed; but in winter the edges of the cut are raised with a knife, and a thin, pliant hard-wood knife or "spud" is pushed around under the bark.

Toasting

After the bark has dropped upon the ground the inside sur-face is warmed with a torch, which softens and straightens it out flat. The torch is made of a bundle of birch bark held in a split stick (Fig. 81).

It is then rolled up like a carpet, with inside surface out, and tightly bound, generally with cedar bark when the latter can be procured (Fig. 80).

If the tree is long enough, a piece is taken off at least nineteen feet in length, so that the ends of the canoe may not be pieced out. A few shorter pieces are wrapped up with the bundle for piecing out the sides.

The Roll

is taken on the back in an upright position, and is carried by a broad band of cedar bark, passing under the lower end of the roll and around in front of the breast and shoulders (Fig. 82).

Effects of Heat

It is laid where the sun will not shine on it and harden it.

Fig. 82.—Mode of carrying roll.

The first effect of heat is to make it pliant. Long exposure to heat or to dry atmosphere makes it hard and brittle.

The Woodwork

is as follows:

Five cross-bars of rock-maple (Figs. 83, 85, and 91). All the rest is of white cedar, taken from the heart. The sap-wood absorbs water, and would make the canoe too heavy, so it is rejected. The wood requires to be straight and clear, and it is best to use perfectly green wood for the ribs.

Two strips $16\frac{1}{2}$ feet long, $1\frac{1}{2}$ inch square, tapering toward either end, the ends being notched (Fig. 83 A) is a section of the 16½ foot strip. Each strip is mortised for the cross-bars (see Fig. 85). The lower outside edge is bevelled off to receive the ends of the ribs.

The dimensions of the cross-bars (Fig. 85) are 12 x 2 x ½ inch, 22½ x 2 x ¾ inch, and 30 x 2 x ⅞ inch. The cross-bars are placed in position, and the ends of the gunwales are tied with spruce

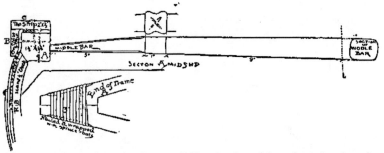

Figs. 83 and 83½.—Showing section of canoe amidship and section and shape of gunwale and top view.

roots after being nailed together to prevent splitting. Each bar is held in place by a peg of hard wood.

For stitching and wrapping, long, slender roots of spruce, or sometimes of elm, are peeled and split in two. Black ash splits are rarely used except for repairing (Figs. 86, 87, 88).

Next we need (B, Fig. 83) two strips 1 or 1¼ inch by ½ inch, a little over 19 feet long, to go outside of gunwales, and (C, Fig. 83) two top strips, same length, 2 inches wide in middle, tapering to 1 inch at either end, 1½ inch thick.

Ribs

About fifty in number (Figs. 91, 92) are split with the grain (F, Fig. 92), so that the heart side of the wood will be on the inner side when the rib is bent. The wood bends better this way. They must be perfectly straight-grained and free from knots.

Ribs for the middle are four inches wide, ribs for the ends about three inches wide (Fig. 91 and G, Fig. 92), and are whittled down to a scant half an inch (Fig. 93). Green wood is generally used, and before it has had any time to season. The ribs may be soft-

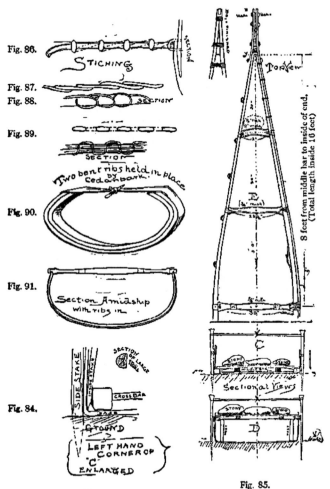

Fig. 86.

STICHING

SECTION

Fig. 87.

Fig. 88.

SECTION

Fig. 89.

SECTION

Two bent ribs held in place by Cedar bark.

Fig. 90.

Fig. 91.

Section Amidship with ribs in.

Fig. 84.

SIDE STAKE

SECTION OF LARGE STONE

CROSS BAR

GROUND

LEFT HAND CORNER OF C ENLARGED

TopView

8 feet from middle bar to inside of end.
(Total length inside 16 feet)

C

Sectional Views

D

Fig. 85.

Details of sticking and framework of canoe.

ened by pouring hot water on them, and should be bent in pairs to prevent breaking (Fig. 90). They are held in shape by a band of cedar bark passed around outside.

The ribs are of importance in the shaping of the canoe. The sides bulge out (Figs. 91, 92). The shape of the ribs determines the depth and stability of the canoe.

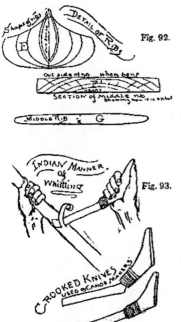

Fig. 92.

Fig. 93.

Details of ribs, Indian knives and method of using them.

Lining Strips

Other strips, an eighth of an inch thick, are carefully whittled out, with straight edges. They are a little over eight feet long, and are designed to be laid inside on the bark, edge to edge, between the bark and the ribs. These strips lap an inch or two where they meet, in the middle of the canoe, and are wider here than at the ends, owing to the greater circumference of the canoe in the middle.

Seasoning

All the timber is carefully tied up before building and laid away. The ribs are allowed to season perfectly, so that they will keep their shape and not spring back.

The Bed

Next the bed is prepared on a level spot, if possible shaded from the sun. A space is levelled about three and a half feet wide and a little longer than the canoe. The surface is made

The Birch-Bark

perfectly smooth. The middle is one or two inches higher than either end.

Building

The frame is laid exactly in the middle of the bed. A small post is driven in the ground (Fig. 94), on which each end of the frame will rest. Stakes, two or three feet long and about two

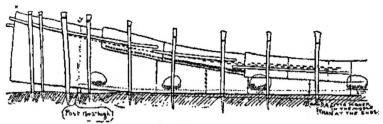

Fig. 94.—Showing stakes supporting bark sides; note stones on the bottom.

inches in diameter, are whittled flat on one side, and are driven with the flat side toward the frame at the following points, leaving a space of about a quarter of an inch between the stake and the frame (Fig. 94): One stake an inch or two on either side of each cross-bar, and another stake half way between each cross-bar. This makes eleven stakes on each side of the frame. Twelve additional stakes are driven as follows: One pair facing each other, at the end of the frame; another pair, an inch apart, about six inches from the last pair, measuring toward the ends of the canoe; and another pair, an inch apart, a foot from these. These last stakes will be nine and a half feet from the middle of the frame, and nineteen feet from the corresponding stakes at the other end. Next, these stakes are all taken up, and the frame laid aside.

To Soften the Bark

Next the bark is unrolled. If it has laid until it has become a little hardened, i' is placed in the river or stream for a day or two. It is spread out flat, and laid upon the bed with the gray or outside surface up. The inside surface is placed downward, and becomes the outside of the canoe.

The frame is replaced upon the bark, so that it will be at the same distance from each side and end of the bed that it was before. At each cross-bar boards are laid across the frame, and heavy stones are laid upon them to keep the frame solid and immovable upon the bark (Fig. 85, C). The edges of the bark are next bent up in a perpendicular position, and in order that it may bend smoothly slits are made in the bark in an outward direction, at right angles to the frame. A cut is made close to the end of each cross-bar, and one half way between each bar, which is generally sufficient to allow the bark to be bent up smoothly. As the bark is bent up, the large stakes are slipped back in the holes which they occupied before, and the tops of each opposite pair are connected with a strip of cedar bark which keeps the stakes perfectly perpendicular. At each end it is necessary to take out a small triangular piece or gore, so that the edges may come together without overlapping.

Next twenty-two pieces of cedar, one to two feet long, and about ½ or ¾ inch thick, are split out, and whittled thin and flat at one end. This sharpened edge is inserted between the outside edge of the frame and the bent-up bark, opposite each large stake. The other end of the chisel-shaped piece is tightly tied to the large stake outside. By means of the *large outside stake* and the inside "*stake*," so-called, the bark is held in a perfectly upright position; and in order to keep the bent-up part more perfectly flat and smooth, the strips of cedar are pushed in lengthwise between the stakes and the bark, on each side of the bark, as shown in sectional views (Fig. 85, C, D).

Sometimes, in place of having temporary strips to go on outside of the bark, the long outside strip (B, Fig. 83), is slipped in place instead.

It may now be seen if the bark is not wide enough. If it is not, the sides must be pieced out with a narrow piece, cut in such a way that the eyes in the bark will run in the same direction as those of the large piece.

As a general rule, from the middle to the next bar the strip for piecing is placed on the inside of the large piece, whose upper edge has previously been trimmed straight, and the two are sewed together by the stitch shown in Fig. 86, the spruce root being passed over another root laid along the trimmed-off edge of the large piece of bark to prevent the stitches from tearing out. From the second bar to the end of the canoe, or as far as may be necessary, the strip is placed outside the large piece, and from the second to the end bar is sewed as in Fig. 87, and from the end bar to the end of the canoe is stitched as in Fig. 88.

Next, the weights are taken off the frame, which is raised up as follows, the bark remaining flat on the bed as before:

A post eight inches long is set up under each end of middle cross-bar (Fig. 85, D), one end resting on the bark and the other end supporting either end of the middle cross-bar. Another post, nine inches long, is similarly placed under each end of the next cross-bar. Another, twelve inches long, is placed under each end of the end cross-bar; and another, sixteen and a half or seventeen inches, supports each end of the frame.

As the posts are placed under each cross-bar, the weights are replaced; and as these posts are higher at the ends than in the middle, the proper curve is obtained for the gunwales. The temporary strips, that have been placed outside the bent-up portion of the bark, are removed, and the long outside strip before mentioned (B, Fig. 83) is slipped in place between the outside stakes and the bark. This strip is next nailed to the frame with wrought-iron nails that pass through the bark and are clinched on the inside. This outside strip has taken exactly the curve of the frame, but its upper edge, before nailing, was raised so as to be out an eighth of an inch (or the thickness of the bark) higher than the top surface of the frame, so that when the edges of the bark have been bent down, and tacked flat to the frame, a level surface will be presented, upon which the wide top strip will eventually be nailed. Formerly the outer strip was bound to the frame with roots every few inches, but now it is nailed.

The cross-bars are now lashed to the frame, having previously been held only by a peg. The roots are passed through holes in the end of the bars, around the outside strip (see right-hand side of Fig. 85). A two-inch piece of the bark, which has been tacked

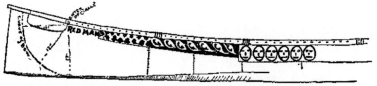

Fig. 95.—Shows how to describe arc of circle for bow, also ornamentation of winter bark.

down upon the frame, is removed at the ends by the cross-bars, where the spruce roots are to pass around, and the outside strip is cut away to a corresponding extent, so that the roots, when wrapped around, will be flush with the surface above.

All the stakes are now removed, and laid away to be ready for the next canoe that may be built, and the canoe taken upside down upon two horses or benches, that will keep the craft clear of the ground.

The shape of the bow is now marked out, either by the eye or with mechancial aid, according to the following rule: An arc of a circle, with a radius of seventeen inches, is described (Fig. 95) having as a centre a point shown in diagram. The bark is then cut away to this line.

Bow-piece

To stiffen the bow, a bow-piece of cedar, nearly three feet long (Fig. 96), an inch and a half wide, and half an inch thick on one edge, bevelled and rounded off toward the other edge, is needed. To facilitate bending edgeways it is split into four or five sections (as in Fig. 98) for about thirty inches. The end that remains unsplit is notched on its thicker edge (Fig. 96) to receive the lower end of an oval cedar board (Fig. 97) that is placed upright in the

The Birch-Bark

bow underneath the tip of the frame. It is bent to correspond with the curve of the boat, with the thin edge toward the outside of the circle, and wrapped with twine, so that it will keep its shape. The bow-piece is placed between the edges of the bark, which are then sewed together by an over-and-over stitch, which passes through the bow-piece.

A pitch is prepared of rosin and grease, in such proportions that it will neither readily crack in cold water nor melt in the sun. One or the other ingredient is added until by test it is found just right.

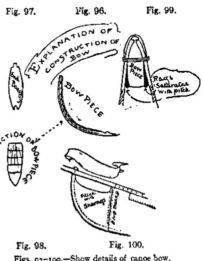

Fig. 97.   Fig. 96.   Fig. 99.

Fig. 98.   Fig. 100.

Figs. 97-100.—Show details of canoe bow.

Patching and Pitching

The canoe is now placed on the ground, right side up, and all holes are covered on the inside with thin birch bark that is pasted down with hot pitch. A strip of cloth is saturated with hot pitch, and pressed into the cracks on either side of the bow-piece inside, between the bark and the bow-piece (Fig. 99).

The thin longitudinal strips are next laid in position, edge to edge, lapping several inches by the middle; they are whittled thin here so as to lap evenly.

The ribs are next tightly driven in place, commencing at the small end ones and working toward the middle. The end ribs may be two or three inches apart, being closer toward the middle, where, in many cases, they touch. Usually, they are about half an inch apart in the middle. Each rib is driven into place with a square-ended stick and a mallet.

Boat-Building and Boating

The ends are stuffed with shavings (Fig. 100 and "Section" Fig. 100½), and an oval cedar board is put in the place formerly occupied by the post that supported the end of the frame. The lower end rests in the notch of the bow-piece, while the upper is cut with two shoulders that fit underneath each side of the frame; Fig. 97 shows the cedar board.

The top strip is next nailed on to the frame. Almost always a piece of bark, a foot or more long, and nine or ten inches wide,

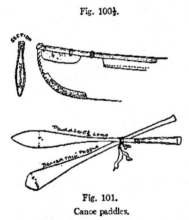

Fig. 100½.

is bent and slipped under, between both top and side strips and the bark. The ends of this piece hang down about three inches below the side strips. The loose ends of the strips are bound together, as in diagram, and the projecting tips of both strips and bow-piece are trimmed off close.

Fig. 101.
Canoe paddles.

Next the canoe is turned upside down. If winter bark has been used, the surface is moistened and the roughness scraped off with a knife. Generally the red rough surface is left in the form of a decorative pattern several inches wide around the upper edge (Fig. 95). Sometimes the maker's name and date are left in this way.

Finally, a strip of stout canvas, three or four inches wide, is dipped in the melted pitch and laid on the stitching at the ends, extending up sufficiently far above the water-line. All cracks and seams are covered with pitch, laid on with a small wooden paddle. While still soft, a wet finger or the palm of the hand is rubbed over the pitch to smooth it down before it hardens.

Leaks

Water is placed inside, and the leaky places marked, to be stopped when dry. A can of rosin is usually carried in the canoe, and when a leak occurs, the canoe is taken out of the water, the

Fig. 101½.—From photograph of Indian building a birch-bark canoe.

leak discovered by sucking, the place dried with a torch of wood or birch bark, and the pitch applied.

Paddles are made of rock maple, and sometimes of birch and even cedar. Bow paddles are usually longer and narrower in the blade than stern paddles (Fig. 101).

Bottom Protection

Sometimes the canoe is shod with "shoes," or strips of cedar, laid lengthwise and tied to the outside of the bark with ash splits that pass through holes in the cedar shoes, and are brought up around the sides of the canoe and tied to each cross-bar. This protects the bottom of the boat from the sharp rocks that abound in some rapid streams.

All canoes are of the general shape of the one described, though this is considerably varied in different localities, some being built with high rolling bows, some slender, some wider, some nearly straight on the bottom, others decidedly curved.

Besides the two paddles the canoe should carry a pole ten feet long, made of a slender spruce, whittled so as to be about one and three-fourths inch in diameter in the middle and smaller at either end, and having at one end either a ring and a spike or else a pointed cap of iron. The pole is used for propelling the canoe up swift streams. This, says Tappan Adney, "is absolutely indispensable." The person using the pole stands in one end, or nearer the middle if alone, and pushes the canoe along close to the bank, so as to take advantage of the eddies, guiding the canoe with one motion, only to be learned by practice, and keeping the pole usually on the side next the bank. Where the streams have rocky and pebbly bottoms poling is easy, but in muddy or soft bottoms it is tiresome work; muddy bottoms, however, are not usually found in rapid waters.

A Canvas Canoe

can be made by substituting canvas in the place of birch bark; and if it is kept well painted it makes not only a durable but a very beautiful boat. The writer once owned a canvas canoe that was at least fifteen years old and still in good condition.

About six yards of ten-ounce cotton canvas, fifty inches wide, will be sufficient to cover a canoe, and it will require two papers of four-ounce copper tacks to secure the canvas on the frame.

The boat should be placed, deck down, upon two "horses" or wooden supports, such as you see carpenters and builders use.

Fold the canvas lengthwise, so as to find the centre, then tack the centre of one end of the cloth to top of bow-piece, or stem, using two or three tacks to hold it securely. Stretch the cloth the length of the boat, pull it taut, with the centre line of the canvas over the keel line of the canoe, and tack the centre of the other end of the cloth to the top of the stern-piece.

If care has been taken thus far, an equal portion of the covering will lap the gunwale on each side of the boat.

The Birch-Bark

Begin amidships and drive the tacks, about two inches apart, along the gunwale and an inch below the deck (on the outside). Tack about two feet on one side, pull the cloth tightly across, and tack it about three feet on the other side. Continue to alternate, tacking on one side and then the other, until finished. With the hands and fingers knead the cloth so as to thicken or "full" it where it would otherwise wrinkle, and it will be possible to stretch the canvas without cutting it over the frame.

The cloth that projects beyond the gunwale may be used for the deck, or it may be cut off after bringing it over and tacking upon the inside of the gunwale, leaving the canoe open like a birch-bark.

To Paddle a Canoe

No one can expect to learn to paddle a canoe from a book, however explicit the directions may be. There is only one way to learn to swim and that is by going into the water and trying it, and the only proper way to learn to paddle a canoe is to paddle one until you catch the knack.

In the ordinary canoe, to be found at the summer watering places, there are cane seats and they are always too high for safety. A top load on any sort of a boat is always dangerous, and every real canoeist seats his passengers on the bottom of the boat and kneels on the bottom himself while paddling. Of course, one's knees will feel more comfortable if there is some sort of a cushion under them, and a passenger will be less liable to get wet if he has a pneumatic cushion on which to sit. No expert canoeist paddles alternately first on the one side, and then on the other; on the contrary, he takes pride in his ability to keep his paddle continuously on either side that suits his convenience.

The Indians of the North Woods are probably the best paddlers, and from them we can take points in the art. It is from them we first learned the use of the canoe, for our open canvas canoes of to-day are practically modelled on the lines of the old birch-barks.

From photographs taken
especially for this book by
Mr. F. K. Vreeland, Camp
Fire Club of America.

Fig. 102.   Fig. 102a.

Fig. 102.—Beginning of stroke. Paddle should not be reached farther forward than this. It is immersed *edgewise* (not point first) with a slicing motion. Note the angle of paddle—rear face of blade turned *outward* to avoid tendency of canoe to turn. Staff of paddle is 6 inches too short. Left hand should be lower.

Fig. 102a.—A moment later. Right hand pushing forward, left hand swinging down. Left hand should be lower on full-sized paddle.

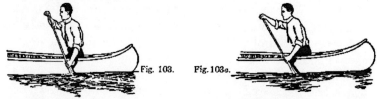

Fig. 103.   Fig. 103a.

Fig. 103.—Putting the power of the body in the stroke by bending slightly forward. Left hand held stationary from now on, to act as fulcrum. The power comes from the right arm and shoulders.

Fig. 103a.—The final effort, full weight of the body on the paddle. The right arm and body are doing the work, the left arm (which is weak at this point) acting as fulcrum. Note twist of the right wrist to give blade the proper angle.

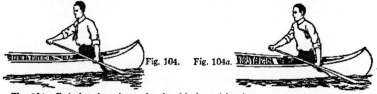

Fig. 104.   Fig. 104a.

Fig. 104.—End of stroke. Arms relaxed and body straightening.

Fig. 104a.—Beginning of recovery. Paddle slides out of water gently. Note that blade is perfectly flat on the surface. No steering action is required. If the canoe tends to swerve it is because the *stroke* was not correct. Only a duffer *steers* with his paddle after the stroke is over. The left hand now moves forward, the right swinging out and back, moving paddle forward horizontally.

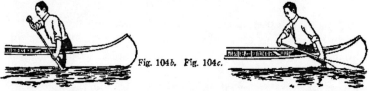

Fig. 104b.   Fig. 104c.

Fig. 104b.—Turning to right. The latter part of a broad sweep outward, away from the canoe. The blade is now being swept toward the canoe, the left hand pulling in, the right pushing out. Position of right wrist shows that blade has the opposite slant to that shown in the straightaway stroke—*i. e.*, the near face of blade is turned *inward*. Blade leaves water with *outer* edge up.

Fig. 104c.—Turning to left. The last motion of a stroke in which the paddle is swept close to the canoe with the blade turned much farther outward than in the straightaway stroke. At end of stroke blade is given an outward sweep, and leaves the water with the *inner* edge up. *This is not a steering* or dragging motion. It is a powerful sweep of the paddle. Note swirl in wake of canoe showing sharp turn

101

The Birch-Bark

When you are standing upright and your paddle is in front of you with the blade upon the ground, the handle should reach to your eye-brows. (See Figs. 101, 102, 103, etc.)

Kneel with the paddle across the canoe and not farther forward than the knees. Then dip the blade *edgewise* (not point first) by raising the upper hand without bending the elbow. Swing the paddle back, keeping it close to the canoe, and give a little twist to the upper wrist to set the paddle at the proper angle shown in the photos. The exact angle depends upon the trim of the boat, the wind, etc., and must be such that the canoe does not swerve *at any part* of the stroke, but travels straight ahead. The lower arm acts mainly as a fulcrum and does not move back and forth more than a foot. The power comes from the upper arm and shoulder, and the body bends forward as the weight is thrown on the paddle. The stroke continues until the paddle slides out of the water endwise, flat on the surface. Then for recovery the blade is brought forward by a swing from the shoulder, *not* lifting it vertically, but swinging it horizontally with the blade parallel to the water and the upper hand low. When it reaches a point opposite the knee it is slid into the water again, edgewise, for another stroke. The motion is a more or less rotary one, like stirring cake, not a simple movement back and forth.

To Carry a Canoe

To pick up a canoe and carry it requires not only the knack but also muscle, and no undeveloped boy should make the attempt, as he might strain himself, with serious results. But there are plenty of young men—good, husky fellows—who can learn to do this without any danger of injury if they are taught *how* to lift by a competent physical instructor.

To pick up a canoe for a "carry," stoop over and grasp the middle brace with the right arm extended, and a short hold with the left hand, as shown in Fig. 105.

When you have a secure hold, hoist the canoe up on your legs, as shown in Fig. 106. Without stopping the motion give her another boost, until you have the canoe with the upper side above your head, as in Fig. 107. In the diagram the paddles are not

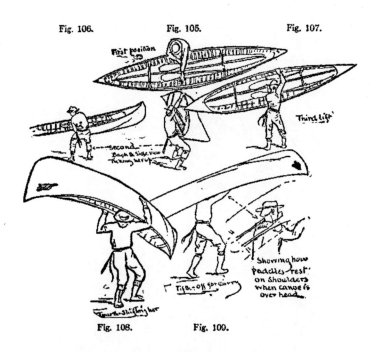

Fig. 106. Fig. 105. Fig. 107.

Fig. 108. Fig. 100.

spread apart as far as they should be. If the paddles are too close together a fall may break ones neck.

Now turn the canoe over your head and slide your head between the paddles (which are lashed to the spreaders, as shown in Fig. 105), and twist your body around as you let the canoe settle down over your head (Fig. 108). If you have a sweater or a coat, it will help your shoulders by making a roll of it to serve as a pad under the paddles, as in Fig. 109. I have seen an Indian carry a canoe in this manner on a dog-trot over a five-mile portage without resting. I also have seen Indians carry canoes over mountains, crossing by the celebrated Ladder Portage in western

THE FIRST TO CROSS
THE LADDER PORTAGE

Fig. 110.—Northern Quebec Indians crossing the "ladder portage."

Quebec, where the only means of scaling a cliff is by ascending a ladder made of notched logs. For real canoe work it is necessary that a man should know how to carry his craft across

Boat-Building and Boating

country from one body of water to another. All through the Lakelands of Canada, and also the Lake St. John district, up to Hudson Bay itself, the only trails are by water, with portage across from one stream or lake to the other.

HOW TO BUILD A PADDLING DORY

A Simple Boat Which Any One Can Build—The Cheapest Sort of a Boat

To construct this craft it is, of course, necessary that we shall have some lumber, but we will use the smallest amount and the expense will come within the limits of a small purse.

First we must have two boards, their lengths depending upon circumstances and the lumber available. The ones in the diagram are supposed to be of pine to measure (after being trimmed) 18 feet long by 18 inches wide and about 1 inch thick. When the boards are trimmed down so as to be exact duplicates of each other, place one board over the other so that their edges all fit exactly and then nail each end of the two boards together for the distance of about six inches. Turn the boards over and nail them upon the opposite side in the same manner, clamping the nail ends if they protrude. Do this by holding the head of a hammer or a stone against the heads of the nails while you hold a wire nail against the protruding end, and with a hammer bend it over the nail until it can be mashed flat against the board so that it will not project beyond its surface.

After you have proceeded thus far, take some pieces of tin (Fig. 112) and bend the ragged edges over, so as to make a clean, straight fold, and hammer it down flat until there are no rough or raw edges exposed. Now tack a piece of this tin over the end of the boards which composed the sides of the boat, as in Fig. 114. Make the holes for the tacks first by driving the pointed end of a wire nail through the tin where you wish the tacks to go and then tack the tin snugly and neatly on, after which tack on another piece of tin on both bow and stern, as in Fig. 116. This will hold the two ends of the boards securely together so that they may be carefully sprung apart in the middle to receive the middle mould which is to hold them in shape until the bottom of the boat is nailed on, and the permanent thwarts, or seats, fastened inside. When the latter are permanently fixed they will keep the boat in shape.

To make the mould, which is only a temporary thing, you may use any rough board, or boards nailed together with cleats

Fig. 111.—Parts of dory.

to hold them. The mould should be 2 feet 6 inches long and 1 foot 4 inches high. Fig. 111 will show you how to cut off the ends to give the proper slant. The dotted lines show the board before it is trimmed in shape. By measuring along the edge of the board from each end 10.8 inches and marking the points, and then, with a carpenter's pencil ruling the diagonal lines to the other edge and ends of the board, the triangles may be sawed off with a hand saw.

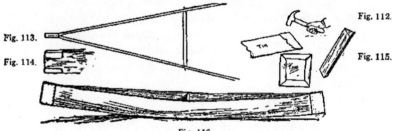

Fig. 112.

Fig. 113.

Fig. 114.

Fig. 115.

Fig. 116.
The simple details of the dory.

Fig. 111 shows where the mould is to be placed in the center of the two side boards. As the boards in this diagram are supposed to be on the slant, and consequently in the perspective, they do not appear as wide as they really are. The diagram is made also with the ends of the side boards free so as to better show the position of the mould. But when the side boards are

How to Build a Paddling Dory

sprung apart and the mould placed in position (Fig. 113), it will appear as in Fig. 116 or Fig. 117. Fig. 115 shows the shape of the stem-posts to be set in both bow and stern and nailed securely in place.

When you have gone thus far fit in two temporary braces near the bow and stern, as shown in Fig. 117. These braces are sim-

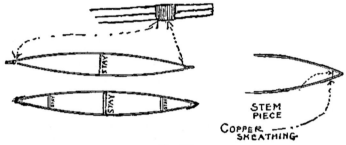

Fig. 118.
Top views of dory and parts of dory.

ply narrow pieces of boards held in position by nails driven through the outside of the boat, the latter left with their heads protruding, so that they may be easily drawn when necessary.

Now turn the boat over bottom up and you will find that the angle at which the sides are bent will cause the bottom boards to rest upon a thin edge of the side boards, as shown in Fig. 119. With an ordinary jack-plane trim this down so that the bottom boards will rest flush and snug, as in Fig. 120.

How to Calk a Boat so That It Won't Leak

If you wish to make a bottom that will never leak,

Fig. 118½.

not even when it is placed in the water for the first time, plane off the boards on their sides, so that when fitted together they will leave a triangular groove between each board, as shown in Fig. 118½. These grooves will show upon the inside of the boat, and not

108

upon the outside, and in this case the calking is done from the inside and not from the outside. They are first calked with candlewick, over which putty is used, but for a rough boat it is not even necessary to use any calking. When the planks swell they will be forced together, so as to exclude all water.

To fasten the bottom on the boat put a board lengthwise at the end, as shown in Fig. 121. One end shows the end board as it is first nailed on, and the other end shows it after it has been trimmed off to correspond with the sides of the boat. Now put your short pieces of boards for the bottom on one at a time, driving each one snug up against its neighbor before nailing it in place and leaving

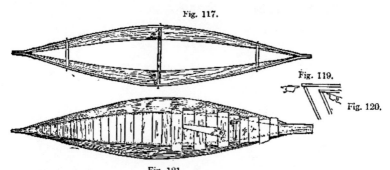

Fig. 117.

Fig. 119.

Fig. 120.

Fig. 121.
Top view with sides in place, also reversed view showing how bottom boards are laid.

the rough or irregular ends of each board protrude on each side, as shown at the right-hand end of Fig. 121.

When all the boards are nailed in place (by beginning at one end and fitting them against each other until the other end is reached) they may be trimmed off with a saw (Fig. 121) and your boat is finished with the exception of the thwarts, or seats.

If you intend to propel this with paddles like a canoe, you will need a seat in the centre for your passenger, and this may be placed in the position occupied by the form (Figs. 111 and 117) after the latter is removed. To fit a seat in it is only necessary to cut two cleats and nail them to the sides of the boat for the seat to rest upon and saw off a board the proper length to fit upon the cleats. It would be well now to fasten the braces in the bow and stern permanently, adjusting them to suit your convenience. The seat should be as low as possible for safety. With this your paddling dory is finished, and may be used even without being painted. A coat of paint, however, improves not only the looks but the tightness and durability of any boat.

We have now advanced so far in our boat-building that it becomes necessary that the beginner should learn more about boats and boating, and since this book is written for beginners, we will take it for granted that they know absolutely nothing about the subject and will give all the rudimentary knowledge for landlubbers in the next chapter.

CANVAS CANOES.

L ONG before the era of boats constructed of boards, and following closely after the primitive attempt at navigation astride a log, and the second step in the form of several logs lashed together, came the intermediate step, by which the form and proportion of a boat was obtained out of comparatively raw material, and without tools. The coracle, as this craft was called, was simply an open frame of basket work, woven from branches and saplings gathered by the riverside, over which the hide of a bullock, or some similar covering, was stretched and sewn; the implements required in constructing such a craft being few and of the simplest form, so that it, in all probability, antedates considerably the canoe fashioned from a hollow log.

This style of boat is still in use, though of course in a greatly improved form, and it still possesses three great advantages, it requires less skill, fewer tools, and less expense of labor and material than any boat of similar excellence. The canvas canoe is usually inferior both in weight, strength and appearance to its wooden rival, but is still a very good boat for all the purposes of the canoeist. The canvas skin is quite heavy when so prepared as to be watertight, and adds nothing to the strength of the boat, which requires, consequently, a stronger frame than a cedar canoe, in which decks and planking add greatly to the strength. If the canoe is of the smaller variety, for paddling only, or carrying but a small sail, it may be built as light or even lighter than a cedar boat of equal stiffness, but if of such a size as 14x30, with 50 to 90ft. of sail, the entire frame must be very strongly braced, and the boat will weigh more than one of cedar.

CANVAS CANOES

The first steps of the building are similar to those previously described for a lapstreak canoe. The moulds are cut out in the same manner, the stem and stern are prepared, a rabbet ½in. deep being cut to take the edge of the canvas. The inner keel, *f*, is ⅜in. thick, 2½ to 3in. wide at middle, and tapers to ¼ at the ends. It is planed up, without a rabbet, and to it the stem *a* and stern *b* are screwed. The outer keel is ⅞in. wide, and as deep as may be desired, not less than ⅞in. It is planed up, the grain pointing aft, as described for a cedar canoe, and is fitted to the scarf of stem, and screwed temporarily to stem, keel and stern, as it must be removed when the canvas is put on.

The frame is now set up on the stocks, the moulds shored in place and all adjusted, then the gunwales *h*, of oak or ash, ¼x¾, are tacked on and jogs or notches are cut in the stem and stern to receive them, leaving their outer surface flush with the surface of the stem and stern. These notches should not be cut across the rabbets. Strips of oak or ash *l l*, 1¼x¼in., are now nailed lightly to the moulds, five or six being used on each side, and the jogs *d d* marked and cut in stem and stern to receive their ends, which, like the gunwales, are secured with screws or rivets to the deadwoods.

The ribs *k* will be of oak or elm, ⅞x¼in. They are planed up, steamed or soaked in boiling water until quite pliable, and then are taken one by one, bent over the knee, and while still hot the middle nailed down to the keel, and then each ribband in turn, from keel to gunwale, is nailed temporarily to the rib with one nail only. Care is necessary to keep the ribbands fair, without hollows or lumps. After all the ribs are in they must be looked over and faired up, the nails being drawn out, if necessary, after which a copper nail is driven through each rib and ribband where they cross, and riveted, making a very strong and elastic frame.

An inwale, *n*, 1x¼in , is now put inside of each gunwale, *h*, being jogged to fit over the heads of the ribs, all three being well riveted together. When this is in, the deck beams *o* may be fitted. They are cut out of oak or hackmatack, 1x⅜in., and are placed as directed for a wooden canoe, the

112

deck frame and coamings being put in in the same manner. The frame is now taken from the stocks, and all corners that might cut the canvas are smoothed and rounded off, then it is painted all over.

The canvas should be hard and closely woven, wide enough to reach from gunwale to gunwale. The frame is first turned upside down, the outer keel removed, and the middle of the canvas fastened along the keel, with a few tacks, then it is turned over, and the canvas drawn tightly over the gunwales. To do this effectively, the two edges of the canvas are laced together, using a sail needle and strong twine, with stitches about 6in. apart along each edge. This lacing is now tightened until the canvas lies flat over the entire frame. At the ends it must be cut neatly, the edge turned in, and tacked tightly in the rabbet, which is first well painted with thick paint. When the ends are finished the lacing is again tightened up, and a row of tacks driven along the gunwale, after which the lacing is removed and the canvas trimmed down, leaving enough to turn in and tack to the inside of the inwale.

The moulds are now removed, and a keelson, *e*, is put in to strengthen the bottom, being of oak, ¾in. deep and 1in. wide. It is slipped in, one or two of the deck beams being removed, if necessary, and the position of each rib marked, then it is removed, and jogs cut to fit down over the ribs, after which it is replaced and screwed down, running far enough forward on the stem to lap well over the scarfs and strengthen it. The deck frame and coaming is next finished, the mast tubes set, and all preparations for decking made as for a wooden canoe. A deck is sometimes laid of ¼in. pine or cedar, over which the canvas is stretched, or the canvas may be laid directly on the beams. The canvas for the deck may be about 6oz. weight, and is stretched tightly down and tacked along the gunwales and around the well. After it is on, half round strips *m m*, are screwed around the edge of the deck, and an outside keel piece of oak ¼in. thick, is fitted to the bottom, the screws passing through into keelson *e*, making all very stiff.

The canvas should now be wetted, and painted with two coats of boiled oil, with a little turpentine and japan dryer mixed in, after which a coat or two of paint of any desired color will finish it off. The paint must be renewed on any spots where it may rub off in use, but the canoe should not be painted oftener than necessary, as its weight is much increased thereby.

Another method of building a canvas boat, as described by a writer in *Forest and Stream*, was to build the boat, of whatever model desired, in the same manner as an ordinary carvel built wooden boat, but using very thin planking, no attempt being made to have the seams in the latter watertight. This frame is then covered with canvas laid in thick paint, causing it to adhere to the wood, and making a smooth, watertight surface. Such a boat can be easily built by those who have not the skill and training necessary to build a wooden boat, and it would be strong and durable, as well as cheap.

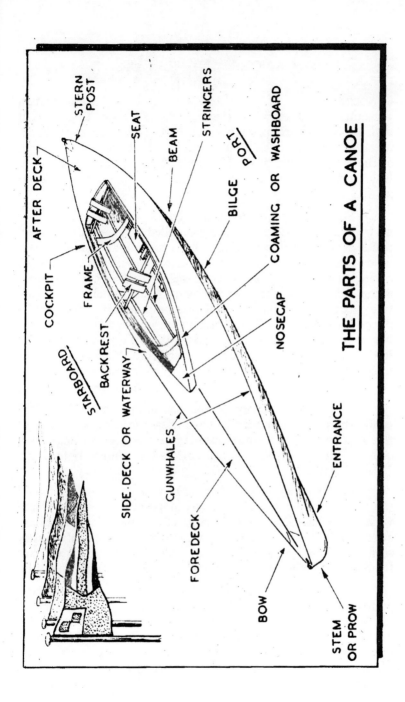

STERN POST

AFTER DECK

SEAT

BEAM

STRINGERS

COCKPIT

FRAME

BACK REST

STARBOARD

SIDE DECK OR WATERWAY

GUNWHALES

FORE DECK

BOW

STEM OR PROW

ENTRANCE

NOSECAP

COAMING OR WASHBOARD

PORT

BILGE

THE PARTS OF A CANOE

CANOES AND KAYAKS

CANOEING is one of the oldest sports. Our ancient British ancestor, sitting astride a floating log and propelling himself with a piece of bark, probably started it. Canoeing, as we know it today, can be considered to have started about the middle of the last century, when McGregor built his canoe, the Rob Roy, and used it to tour the waterways of Europe and even further afield.

The Rob Roy (*fig.* 1*a*) was a light all-wood canoe, decked in with a small cockpit, and propelled by a double-bladed paddle. McGregor's writings of his tours made many others follow and canoeing became extremely popular. It is worth noting that all this pioneer work was British. There has been a common impression that canoeing is a German, or at any rate a continental sport, which has only recently been introduced into England. True, much development in recent years has been continental, but we started it and, even at the begining of this century, canoeing by any but Britishers was so uncommon on the continent that a German canoer in his own country was usually greeted as an "Englander".

From the popularity of the paddling type of Rob Roy canoe there developed a fashion for sailing canoes. Some of the rigs become so complicated and the cost so high that canoeing as a popular sport suffered a slump before the 1914-18 war.

The Canadian canoe (*fig.* 1*b*), with its open hull and upturned ends, has kept a steady popularity throughout the years. It is based on the Red Indian birch bark design. There are a number of methods of construction, but the craft mostly seen in this country have skins made of narrow planks laid flush and stiffened by light ribs placed close together laterally.

The greatest increase in the popularity of canoeing came with the introduction of the folding canoe (*fig.* 1*c*) after the 1914-18 war. Obviously, a craft which can be packed into a couple of bags and carried about, yet when assembled carries two people and all their camping kit, has considerable possibilities—and it is this type of craft which most modern canoers use.

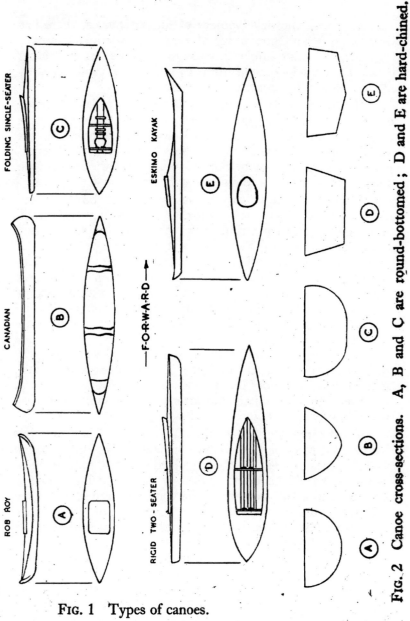

FIG. 1 Types of canoes.

FOLDING SINGLE-SEATER

CANADIAN

ROB ROY

ESKIMO KAYAK

RIGID TWO-SEATER

←F-O-R-W-A-R-D→

FIG. 2 Canoe cross-sections. A, B and C are round-bottomed; D and E are hard-chined.

Alongside the development of folding canoes, there has been a growth in popularity of rigid canvas covered canoes (*fig. 1d*), which are similar in appearance to the erected folding craft. They can be bought from any makers and can be cheaply made at home by amateur craftsmen.

It is probably true that 90% of canoeing today is carried out in the folding or rigid decked canoes of the type shown in the frontispiece. If the reader has any doubt about the strength and practicability of such an apparently fragile craft, perhaps the author may be allowed to drop into the first person and briefly describe a few of his own expeditions.

Many years ago, two of us youngsters built a rigid canvas-covered two-seater canoe, using packing case wood and other second-hand timber for the frame and an old shop blind for the skin. The whole cost was not much over £1. During a summer holiday we sent the canoe, packed with camping kit to Glasbury-on-Wye by goods train. From there we journeyed down the Wye, camping at night and thoroughly enjoying ourselves : most of the time far away from civilisation and in close touch with nature. The rapids on this river are not dangerous, but they gave us plenty of thrills. To negotiate a rapid, with the boiling water surging around you and spray flying over the decks, then to glide into the slack water below, is a thrill which must be experienced to be appreciated—in fact we liked it so much that after shooting some rapids we towed the boat back and went down again.

Most canoers complete their Wye trip at Chepstow, but we decided to cross the Bristol Channel and go up the Avon to our homes in Bristol. This involved about 10 miles of open estuary. We left the mouth of the Wye in a flat calm, but when we were about half way across the wind began to blow against the tide, and soon there was a nasty chop, with waves which were certainly frightening at first—then we realised that our craft seemed to be more confident than we were. Providing we met the largest waves more or less head-on we kept dry. Occasionally, we were unlucky and shipped a little water (we had no spray covers), but when we arrived at Avonmouth and a harbour official, who had been watching us, told us that the wind was force 8 (a gale), we felt extremely pleased with ourselves, despite our wet pants.

If that sounds too strenuous for you, and your inclination is towards a lazy holiday, perhaps this tempts you :

My wife and I took a folding canoe and camping kit to Cricklade in Gloucestershire. The whole lot went as personal luggage on the train. From there we spent a leisurely three weeks travelling down the Thames ; first of all through the beautiful rural stretches above Oxford, then past the well-known beauty spots on the more popular reaches, and finally down the tidal river from Teddington, right through the heart of London to finish at Greenwich. We were completely independent. If we liked a place we stopped there two nights. If we fancied a bed instead of camping we stopped at a riverside inn. If there was a breeze we hoisted a sail and let the wind do the work, while we stretched out in the cockpit.

I could tell you too of trips on continental rivers or around our coast. Or again, of odd week-ends when we have selected a blue line on an Ordnance Survey map, then strapped the folding canoe on the back of the car and explored streams so tiny that probably no other craft had ever floated on them. However, the main purpose of this book is to help you to make a start at canoeing, and we must get back to business.

THE KAYAKS

Both the folding and rigid decked canoes have as their ancestor the Eskimo kayak (*fig.* 1e)—a slim round-bottomed craft into which the occupant laced himself. It fitted him. so closely that he might almost be said to be wearing it. In this craft the Eskimo fished and hunted in the Arctic regions— and still does. Folding canoes on traditional kayak lines have been built, and in them experts are able to perform the "Eskimo roll"—a complete roll over, under the water and return to upright at the opposite side. These craft, however, are only for sport, touring craft being beamier and roomier. It is common to refer to a folding craft as a canoe and a rigid craft as a kayak, although the latter is not built on Eskimo lines.

The underwater section and the method of forming the skin of the canoe, or any other craft, are important.

119

A round-bottomed boat is one in which a cross-section of the hull is a curve. A curve of a midship section which forms part of a circle (*fig. 2a*) is unstable. A V-shaped curve is even worse (*fig. 2b*), but both of these shapes may be found in craft designed solely for racing. The best cross-section for a touring canoe is D-shaped (*fig. 2c*). There should be a good width of almost flat floor at the centre.

Some canoes are "hard-chined", i.e. there is an angle between the sides and the bottom. The bottom itself may be flat, in which case the hull has a "flattie" cross-section (*fig 2d*), or in the form of a shallow V, called a "sharpie" cross-section (*fig. 2e*). A dead flat bottom is more suitable for a heavily constructed knockabout boat for a pleasure lake or the seaside than for touring. Titcraft canoes have V-shaped bottoms and flat sides.

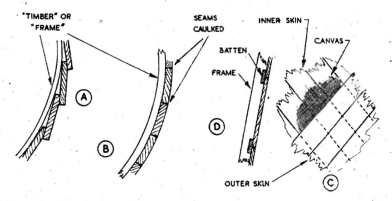

FIG. 3   Typical methods of planking : A, clinker ; B, carvel ; C, double diagonal ; D, seam-batten carvel.

Craft constructed wholly of wood may be of clinker construction, with the planks lapped over each other and laid fore and aft (*fig. 3a*) ; carvel construction, with the planks fore and aft, but flush (*fig. 3b*) ; double diagonal, with two skins of diagonal planking separated by painted canvas (*fig 3c*) ; or seam-batten construction, with wide thin planks laid similarly to carvel, but with the joints covered inside by battens (*fig. 3d*).

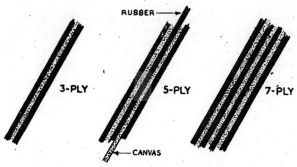

FIG. 4   Sections of folding canoe skins.

Canvas-covered craft have a built-up framework of widely-spaced laths, over which the canvas is stretched and made waterproof by treating with oil and paint.   Some Canadian canoes are built almost in the same way as for wood-only construction, but the joints are not so carefully fitted, then the whole hull is covered with canvas.

Folding canoes are covered by rubberised fabric. This is made in the form of a ply—three, five or seven (*fig.* 4). Five ply is commonest. The outer rubber layer is thickest, and two kinds of canvas are used, one coarse for toughness and one fine for strength.

The choice of canoe is dependent on a number of conditions and must be decided by the individual. Experience will bring personal preferences, and for that reason it is as well to buy a comparatively cheap canoe at first, possibly secondhand, and discard it in favour of one which suits your own specification when you have had enough experience to decide on your particular needs.

CANADIAN CANOES, propelled traditionally by single-bladed paddles, are best suited for permanent use on one river. For riverside dwellers and others with suitable mooring or storage facilities they are ideal for outings of a day or so in settled weather.   Their bulk makes them awkward and expensive to transport to other waterways. It is unusual to fit any sort of cover to a Canadian canoe, so, when touring, everything has to be packed in waterproof bags. The crew also need full waterproof kit.

At first it may be thought that all Canadian canoes are alike. This is far from the case. In America, where these craft still have considerable commercial use, an enormous variety of sizes and sections are available, it being possible to state a purpose and have a canoe built to measure.

When selecting a canoe for general purposes, pick one with a fairly wide beam and with the flatness at the centre extending well fore and aft. Most Canadian canoes are imported from America. One of the commonest and best makes is the "Peterborough".

RIGID KAYAKS. A rigid canvas-covered craft is usually chosen for its cheapness. An amateur carpenter, with only average ability, can successfully build a two-seater craft for about £3. While cheapness is the usual reason for choosing a rigid kayak, it should also be remembered that when speed is the aim, a rigid canoe can be designed to beat a folding craft. Certain requirements of assembly and dismantling prevent the latter having the best possible lines.

The rigid kayak suffers from the disadvantage of its bulk when transporting it, but the difficulty is not as acute as might be imagined. For transport by goods train, the charges are by weight only, bulk being ignored ; and despite its size, a 17ft. two-seater weighs considerably under 100 lbs. The author has sent a kayak of this size to a number of canoeable

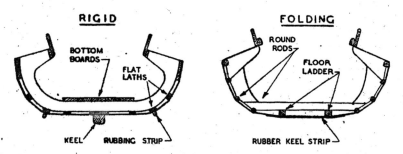

FIG. 5 Comparative cross-sections of folding and rigid canoes. Note the protective rubbing strips.

rivers, and each time the kayak has travelled safely, being given a truck to itself, and cost only a few shillings per hundred miles. A single-seater will travel inverted on top of a moderate-sized car, or a trailer can be used.

The canvas covering of a kayak is not as strong as the rubberised fabric of the folding canoe, but good canvas will stand plenty of wear, particularly if, as is usual, an outside keel and rubbing strips are fitted (*fig.* 5). With hard use a canvas skin will stand up to it for four or five years. It is then not a very expensive or difficult job to re-cover the framework.

Besides the canvas-covered kayak there have been a number of similar-shaped craft made in other materials.

The original Rob Roy was all wood, the hull itself being clinker-built. Several boat hiring stations have canoes of this build for hire. Galvanised iron and aluminium alloys have been used, and, despite their apparent unsuitability, they have made satisfactory craft. Moulded plywood construction can produce a hull of perfect lines. Unfortunately, some canoes in the past have been made of plywood in which the cement used has not been fully waterproof. The unsatisfactory results of this have given plywood a bad name, but with the development of absolutely waterproof synthetic resin cement there is nothing to fear in the use of modern waterproof plywood. Many of the small craft used in the war were built almost entirely of waterproof plywood.

SEMI-FOLDING CANOES. A number of ways of reducing the size of a canoe for stowing or transport has been tried as alternative to the method of fully dismantling used in the folding canoe proper. Titcraft canoes consist basically of two planks, forming the sides, to which are attached a canvas bottom and the canvas decking. These planks are joined at the ends and the canoe is given shape by spreaders, which force the sides apart. To pack the canoe, the spreaders are taken out and the whole thing reduces to about 3 ins. thick.

Another idea is the making of the canoe in three sections, each rigid and watertight—one forming the cockpit and the others the tapered decked ends. For use the three parts are bolted together, while for packing, the ends fit inside the cockpit portion.

FOLDING CANOES. Most modern canoers use this type of craft. The skin is of rubberised fabric and the deck, which is sewn to it, is of stout canvas. The framework consists of an arrangement of round wooden rods, which join together with brass sleeves. The backbone of the craft is a ladder-like arrangement along the centre of the bottom, which tensions and stiffens the boat and carries the seats. Shape is given laterally by removable frames. Finally, around the cockpit is a wooden coaming, to which are attached the backrests.

The whole, despite its apparent fragility and flexibility, makes an enormously strong craft, which can safely be used at sea, yet is of such shallow draught that it will almost float on a bit of damp ground! The English Channel has been crossed in a folding canoe so often that a trip does not call for comment. Captain Romer crossed the South Atlantic in one in 90 days.

There is ample stowage space under the decks and the carrying capacity is unbelievable to the uninitiated. Folding canoes, very little different from the standard types, used for Commando and Naval work during the war, carried mines ' wireless transmitters, generating plants and other heavy gear along with fully-equipped crews, often operating from base ships 10 miles out at sea. One maker quotes his Sports-tourer two-seater model as having a capacity of 800 lbs., the Lightweight two-seater carries 550 lbs. and the popular single-seater 300 lbs.

Most makers supply a variety of canoes, not only with various seating capacities, but with varying lengths. An increase in length usually makes for a faster boat, but the shorter craft is, naturally, more compact to pack. Typical details of popular types are :—

Short two-seater : Length 14 ft. 9 ins. Beam 2 ft. 6 ins.
Cockpit 5 ft. by 1 ft. 8 ins.
Weight 50 lbs.

Sports-tourer
. Two-seater : Length 17 ft. 9 ins. Beam 2 ft. 8 ins.
Cockpit 7 ft. 11 ins. by 1ft. 9 ins.
Weight 68 lbs.

Popular single seater :	Length 11 ft. Beam 2 ft. 4 ins. Cockpit 3 ft. 4 ins. by 1 ft. 6 ins. Weight 30 lbs.
Sports single-seater :	Length 14 ft. 9 ins. Beam 2 ft. 2 ins. Cockpit 5 ft. by 1ft. 4 ins. Weight 45 lbs.

Although each maker has his own way of arranging particular fittings and each may offer something special in his own boats, the method of erecting folding canoes is generally much the same for all makes.

When you first receive a folding canoe and turn out the contents of the bags, the collection of bits and pieces which confronts you will, to say the least, be a little breathtaking. However, get somewhere on your own, away from an audience, then, with the aid of the maker's instruction booklet go ahead calmly (*fig.* 6). The first erection may take you a couple of hours, but do not let that worry you. After a very little practice you will be doing it in under 20 minutes.

The best place to work is on a smooth lawn. In any case, avoid such things as broken bottles and sharp stones. Roll out the hull, decking uppermost. Select the bow and stern assemblies, which are end pieces with some rods attached. Lay them alongside the appropriate parts of the hull. Notice that many parts have numbers indicating where they go and may have ends marked "bow" or "stern" to show direction. The two loose parts of the floor ladder clip or bolt to the end assemblies. Loose round rods should be attached to the rods marked to mate with them. The appropriate cross-frames should be clipped into place where marked.

Most of the framework will now be assembled in two halves. Stand astride the hull and ease the stern framework into place. Do the same with the bow assembly.

At this stage the parts will overlap at the centre, but that does not matter. On one half of the centre ladder there is a hinged portion. This mates with its opposite half, which is lifted to join it. Check that everything is clear inside at

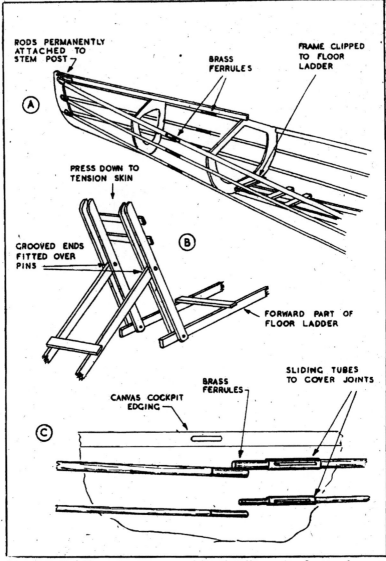

FIG. 6 Folding canoe assembly details. A, forward part assembled ready for insertion in skin. B, tensioning device at junction of floor ladder parts. C, the meeting ends of the round stringers near the centre of the canoe. Each pair must be sprung together and joined by the sliding tube.

each end, then force the hinged portion down and clip the parts together. This will force the framework well into the ends. Spring the mating round rods together and join them with the brass sleeves.

The boat will now have taken shape and it only remains to slip in the other frames, fix the coaming (or "washboards" as some makers call them), seats and backrests. It is in the fitting of these final parts that makers differ, but the method should be fairly obvious.

A folding canoe will last for years, even if abused, but if care is taken over its maintenance, its life may be doubled. The rubberised skin is the vital part. The wood and metal parts will look after themselves, providing any bare wood is re-varnished and the brass parts cleaned and smeared with vaseline.

When the boat is erected and in use little harm will come to the rubber, providing it is washed off with clean water and occasionally treated with the preservatives which the makers supply. It is in storage that care is needed. If the skin is left rolled up in its bag for a few weeks between trips it will not matter, providing it is dry. It is during the long period of storage through the winter that deterioration may occur.

Rubber is adversely affected by extremes of heat or cold, but will last a long time in moderate temperatures. The canoe should, therefore, not be stored in a heated room or in an exposed outhouse. Limits of space will govern how the canoe can be stored. If possible it should be erected and left with any tensioning devices slackened off. The author's own canoe spends its winters in this manner, resting across the ceiling joists in the attic.

If space is limited, the skin may be stored off the framework. Its ends should be stuffed with paper and turned in towards the centre. The important thing is to avoid sharp kinks in the skin. If storage, even in this way, takes up too much room, the skin may be kept folded in its bag. Newspapers should be placed between the folds, and the rubber sprinkled plentifully with French chalk to prevent sticking.

CHAPTER V.

THE ROB ROY CANOE.

In this chapter it is proposed to show how to build a Rob Roy canoe, giving its dimensions and mentioning its peculiarities. Everyone knows that a canoe is only a modified boat reduced to its smallest dimensions, and it is, in fact, very much the same as the skiff just described to build, with the exception that it requires much more careful work, because, as it is small, the parts will not stand the same " dodging " in the event of an error being made.

There are many kinds of canoes made, though they are all on the same principle ; some of them are intended for sailing purposes, and are, therefore, made so large, and have such a weight of ballast, that they are really boats in every respect, retaining a sort of fancied resemblance to the justly celebrated Rob Roy. The beauty of a canoe is its extreme simplicity and yet efficiency, so that when a great complexity is produced with sliding keels, topmasts, rudders, mizenmasts, &c., all the quality of this kind of boat disappears. Besides which, the portability of a canoe is, or should be, a leading feature, and not in any way to be despised.

Of the different kinds of canoes that have been brought out since the introduction of the Rob Roy, none have really surpassed it for general travel, though in special descriptions of travel there are some which are superior. For instance, the bluff lines of a Rob Roy make it a rather heavy craft to paddle against the current of a fairly swift stream, and so here a Ringleader has advantages ; but the Ringleader is not nearly so handy as the Rob Roy on account of its great length—viz., 17ft. 6in., and some have been made as long as 22ft. For this reason it is not nearly so quickly turned, but it was claimed to stand rough water better, which, however, has never been really proved. The Nautilus, which is the other variety which is most adopted, is a decided improvement on the Ringleader, standing very rough water much better and is far more manageable, but it has the same disadvantage as the Rob Roy in being heavier to paddle. All these varieties have, in their turn, given birth to many others, and there are at least eleven distinct varieties of the original canoe, besides a great number of nondescript arrangements, used for fast or peculiar work, as racing and sporting. In a manual like this, where only a few pages can be devoted to one particular craft, it would be impossible to describe all the varieties ; but for general work an ordinary Rob Roy is best.

A good Rob Roy should weigh from 50lb. to 60lb., and, by a careful selection of material, the amateur can be fairly sure of attaining this lightness. Of course, in canoe building the best materials alone should be used, and it is now generally admitted that oak most fully answers the requirement. Very good canoes may be built in cedar, teak, mahogany, and pine for the skin ; but, except cedar and pine, they are not much used. If, however, the amateur is anxious to build a very light and strong canoe, and has the skill and the patience to work in thin material, there is no wood to be got in the English wood market that will excel teak. In selecting his material, let the amateur pick out good sound white oak, straight in the grain for the skin. This must be a bare quarter of an inch thick, so as to plane down to a good 3-16ths of an inch, and it must be 4½in. wide. For the keel and stem and stern posts he will also want oak, and for the decking cedar (red) ½in. thick. He will also require some thin spruce or red pine of a bare 3-8ths of an inch for floor boards and back board. Copper nails of 17 gauge and copal boat varnish must be used.

The chief dimensions of the canoe that is proposed for the amateur to build are as follows :

Length over all, 12ft. 6in.
Length on load-water line, 12ft.
Beam on load-water line, which is also the greatest beam, 2ft. 2in.
Beam at level of the gunwale, 2ft.
Depth inside at midship, 9in.
Depth inside at the ends, 12in.
Camber, 1in.
Distance of midship from the bows, 7ft. 1in.
Proportion of length of beam of the fore section is as 6½ is to 1.

Fig. 43 gives a sheer plan and plan of the canoe. In this the dotted line *a* shows the position of the midship frame in relation to the rest of the boat, and *c* and *b* of the bow and stern frames, which are respectively 3ft. 6in. and 2ft. 9in. from the midship frame. A shows the position of the hole in the stem for the tow-line, which must be ½in. in diameter, and B shows the socket for the mast. In the plan the dotted lines show the position of the beams to support the deck, while those in the sheer view show the position of the floor. The hatchway is 36in. long and 18in. wide. ·

It is hardly necessary to repeat in detail all the processes in building a canoe, because, as before explained, they are similar to that required for a skiff, therefore only the more complex portions will be described. The keel must be made of oak, cut out of the solid, as is shown in Fig. 19, Chapter IV., and its dimensions are as follows : For the wood, have in the rough a piece of oak 1½in. by 2¾in., by 12ft. long ; and the dimensions this has to be dressed to are : ¾in. outside keel, with a ½in. face, with a ¼in. semi-circular groove cut in it, as is shown in Fig. 44 at A, which is afterwards to receive the keel band, as shown.

The rabbets for the planking are $\frac{1}{4}$in. wide by 3-8ths of an inch deep. From this drawing and the dimensions the amateur will be

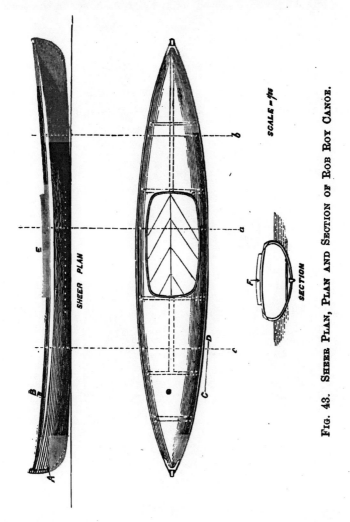

FIG. 43. SHEER PLAN, PLAN AND SECTION OF BOB ROY CANOE.

able to proportion the rest of the keel as in the skiff. In a small boat like this the amateur may vary his practice for fitting the posts, and in Figs. 45 and 46 he will find two plans which answer very well but require nice work.

In Fig. 45 a wedge shaped joint, as at A, is cut in the posts.

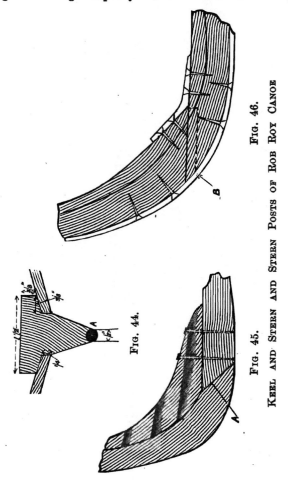

Fig. 46.

Fig. 44.

Fig. 45.

Keel and Stern and Stern Posts of Rob Roy Canoe.

Two good screws, or three if the joints are very long, hold the posts in their places, the wedge preventing all rise of the posts on striking a stone. In Fig. 46 the keel is carried right forward, and the post lies on the top of it, as shown at B. Between the posts and the keel a small tenon is cut, which prevents all twisting movement of the post, while a small .copper or galvanised angle iron at the back and the keel band, which in this case must be broad and flat, holds the post tight to the keel. The angle iron and keel band must, of course, be screwed on and not nailed. The fixing of these posts in a canoe is far more important than those of a skiff, because a skiff is not expected to get bumped about, but this is very often the regular order of things for a canoe, especially if its owner is fond of running rapids or navigating on shallow streams. For these reasons the bow or fore foot of a canoe should always be very well rounded, so that on striking a rock it may rise on to it and not ram it. Both the plans shown are very good for meeting strains caused by this class of work, that shown in Fig. 46 being well suited for canoes of great rise of fore foot.

The heel or foot of the stern post should be fitted just the same as the fore foot, unless it is put in square, in which case it may be fitted as shown in Fig. 23, page 54.

In a canoe the ribs may be similar in design to those in a skiff, but the dimensions must be smaller. In oak ribs cut out of the piece to shape—say, $\frac{5}{8}$in. by $\frac{3}{8}$in.—spaced every twelve inches with half ribs midway between ; and for bent pine ribs— say, $\frac{1}{4}$in. thick by $\frac{5}{8}$in. wide—spaced every ten inches. A canoe may always have an extra rib or so spaced in about the swell of its length—as at C to D in the plan of Fig. 43—which helps it vastly in all work amongst rocky rivers.

The decks strengthen a canoe exceedingly—in fact, if it were not for the decks or some equivalent brace they could not stand the knocking about to which they are subjected. A more elastic material, like the cedar and birch bark of Canadian canoes, would be required. Supposing all the canoe built except the decking, and that the inside has received two good coats of varnish, the amateur must proceed to deck it. To do this he must put in the frames shown by the dotted lines in Fig. 43, and then dress out his cedar to shape. The frames mentioned must be nicely mortised in; it is the best way, though knees may be used. Having procured this cedar, which should be broad enough to cover in the half of the decking at its widest part, all dressed to shape, he must tack it down with copper tacks, spaced every half inch all along the gunwale and the frames to support the deck. The deck should be in not more than four pieces—one for the fore end, one ditto for the stern, and one for each side of the hatchway. This being finished, a strip of very thin clear-grained oak or ash must be obtained—$1\frac{1}{4}$in. wide, $1\frac{1}{8}$in. thick, and about 9ft. to 10ft. long. This must be bent round the inside edge of the hatchway, and nailed to the decking as a coaming, standing $\frac{3}{4}$in. above the deck, as is shown in E (Fig. 43.) It is not probable that the amateur can do this all in one piece, so he had better cut it in two, so as to get the joints on the centre line of the canoe on the highest portion of the deck, as at F (Fig. 43). The amateur will have to soften this piece, as was described in Chapter IV.

The amateur must now proceed to fit his canoe with the various iron plates, &c., necessary. The bow and stern should each have a nose of iron or copper, copper being that usually used, as in Fig. 34, p. 64. A flat plate of copper may also be advantageously used in each corner of the hatchway, holding the joints of the deck and the coaming together. Also two small brass cleets might be put on, one on each side of the hatchway, to secure the rigging cords to, and a brass socket for the mast must be screwed on.

Fig. 47 illustrates the sails and rigging, &c. In this A is the outline of the lugsail; this sail is made of wide cotton sheeting,

G

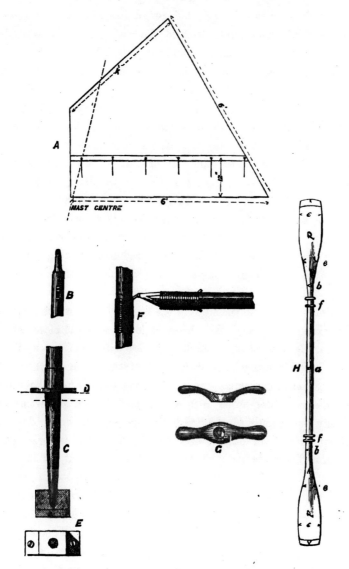

FIG. 47. SAIL, PADDLE, AND FITTINGS OF ROB ROY CANOE.

so that it is all in one piece, but round the edge is sewn stout cotton cord; and across, to hold the reefing lines on each side, sewn strong broad tape. No two canoeists have the same arrangement of sails; so this is only given as a guide to help the amateur to get the right proportions. In the matter of sails and cordage he will find nothing better than cotton for both. B shows the mast head, which is 1in. in diameter, and has a small blind pulley sheaf let into it. This arrangement answers better than a block. C shows the tail or foot of the mast between decks, and D the brass socket screwed to the deck, Where the mast enters the socket it is 2in. in diameter, tapering from the 1in. at the top to ¾in. at the foot. The taper should be very gradual, the mast being almost of the same diameter at 12in. from the socket as there, and then gradually tapering down to the pulley in a gentle curve. The total length of the mast is 5ft. 8in., and it should be made of ash or rock elm. E is a section and plan of the step for the foot of the mast, and should be made of a piece of oak, either nailed on to a flat piece, which in turn is screwed on to the keel, or else cut out of the block in one. F illustrates the attachment of the boom to the mast. This is made by taking a piece of strong soft leather, about 9in. long, and lashing it on with strong sail thread, or fine string, firmly and evenly to the mast and end of the boom, leaving about an inch of play between them. This answers every purpose, and is exceedingly simple and strong, and not liable to get out of order. The boom may be of 1in., tapering to ¾in., ash or rock elm, 6ft. 3in. long. G illustrates one of the cleets, which were mentioned as being screwed on to the decks, one on each side of the hatchway. H illustrates the paddle. This may be made of red pine or black birch. Its dimensions are as follow : Diameter at *a*, 1¼in.; ditto at *b b*, ¾in.; width at *c c*, 6in.; ditto at *e e*, 3in.; length at *d d*, 15in.; total length, 6ft. 6in.

G 2

PRACTICAL BOAT BUILDING.

The end is banded with copper, and there are on each end, at *f f*, two round indiarubber rings to catch the water that may drop down. The blades should be painted, and the whole paddle varnished.

In varnishing his work the amateur should allow as much time as possible between the time of putting on each coat, and especially the last, as the wood does not absorb the varnish so readily after receiving the first coat. It is also a point to put on the varnish as thin as possible. It is better and more satisfactory to put on an extra coat than to put one on thick, as the varnish dries much harder in the former case. When everything is finished, the outside of the canoe should receive two coats of varnish, and, when they are dry, all the canoe which is get-at-able should receive another, which is a final one, the canoe being quite finished when this is dry.

In this chapter on canoes but little mention has been made of dimensions, as it is impossible to enter into all the details that would be necessary to do so; but, as premised in the earlier portion of the subject, the amateur who undertakes to build a boat must have some knowledge of material and proportion. If, however, the amateur will take the proportions of the skiff, and reduce them by one-third, he will not be very far out. For nails, 1in. to 1½in. will do, except at the extreme ends, where 1½in. to 2in. are better.

THE PADDLE

THE proper paddle is essential for accurate, easy, and strong propulsion of a canoe. Though a most important feature in canoeing, comparatively little consideration is given to the selection of a paddle, even by experienced canoemen.

Paddles are made of spruce, cedar, maple, ash, and pine. The paddle most generally furnished by canoe manufacturers is made of spruce or maple. Cedar, ash, and pine paddles are generally those made by Indians for their own use.

The canoeing paddle is a single-bladed affair, although the double-bladed arrangement, usually eight and one-half to ten feet long, is sometimes used. The most efficient work is done with the single-bladed paddle, and its use is practically universal.

The first consideration in the selection of a paddle is the length. The accepted rule is that the paddle should be as long as the user is tall. This is true if paddling is done from a seat. In paddling from the knees, the paddle may be three inches shorter, though the full length is better. The rule does not apply to bow paddlers. In that position, especially if paddling is done from the knees, the implement should be three inches shorter than the height of the paddler. A bow paddler can work with a paddle a foot shorter than he is tall, but the stern man has difficulty if the paddle is six inches shorter than his height.

Two woods, spruce and maple, are chiefly used. Paddles made of spruce are thick, strong, and light. They are also very unyielding. Paddles of maple are heavy, strong, and with a certain amount of spring. The spruce paddle wears and frays quickly if used in rapids, for breaking ice in the fall, or if used for poling in shallow water. The ragged edge must be trimmed often, an operation which continually reduces the size of the blade. The spruce paddle, also because of its thickness and softness, does not enter or leave the water silently or freely.

The best paddle for all-round use is that made of maple. There is a tendency on the part of manufacturers, however, to produce a paddle too thick and heavy. Such paddles have all the deficiencies of the spruce paddle, excepting wear, without the advantage of being light, and they do not have sufficient spring.

The maple paddle will stand much more abuse, especially when used as a pole or in rapids, and the strength of the wood permits a thin blade that enters and leaves the water cleanly. Because of the heaviness of the material, the maple paddle should be made from the finest straight-grained wood, that the lightest, thinnest implement consistent with strength may be possible. The usual paddle does not come up to such a standard.

For long cruises in the wilderness the maple paddle is the superior. The spruce paddle, in fact, because of its stiffness, is entitled to a place only in a racing canoe.

The experienced canoeist always tests the " spring " of a paddle the moment he picks it up. For racing, the stiff, unyielding blade is desirable, but for the grind of an all-day journey, a paddle that " gives " softens the shock of quick, hard strokes. The advantage of a " springy " paddle is also felt in the recovery. If the paddle is given a final snap at the end of a stroke, the spring of the blade will shoot it forward for the next stroke with little effort on the part of the paddler.

Paddles are made with blades of several shapes, the design varying with the district. The size of the blade is of more importance. Too large a blade makes the work too heavy; too small a blade results in wasted energy. A large blade is held almost stationary in the water, and the shock and strain on arms and shoulders are too severe. For the opposite reason, a small blade does not remain stationary in the water and does not afford a sufficient purchase for efficient propulsion or handling.

The size of the blade, of course, must depend upon the size and strength of the paddler. For the usual canoeist a blade five and one-half inches wide and two feet eight or ten inches long is sufficient.

Manufactured paddles invariably are made with a knob or grip at the end of the shaft for the upper hand. Many Indians make paddles with straight, tapering shafts. While their mode of paddling makes the straight shaft preferable, there is still a question as to the grip being essential to a white man. In any event, he can often ease strained muscles by grasping the shaft below the grip, the thumb side of the hand being nearer the blade and the back of the hand toward the paddler. Paddles made by canoe manufacturers invariably are varnished. While this adds to the life of the paddle, it is hard on the hands. If one has a varnished paddle it is better to scrape the varnish from the shaft at the points where it is grasped. The natural wood will not blister so badly. An oiled paddle absorbs water after a time and becomes heavier. This can be avoided if the application of oil is renewed occasionally.

Any paddle, varnished or oiled, should not be left in the sun, especially after it has been long in the water. It will check, or split. Paddles should be watched and the tips trimmed when they become ragged.

An emergency paddle should always be carried. On a long trip it is essential and should be placed always within easy reach of the stern paddler. Then, in case of accident, either in rips or a heavy sea, he need not miss a stroke. Even on a sunset paddle, an emergency blade will come in handy should the one in use be dropped or broken.

TYPES OF CANOES; THEIR CONSTRUCTION

SO far as construction and materials are concerned, canoes are made in three types— the wooden, canvas, and birchbark. The birch bark will drown the other two, but it is slower, more difficult to handle, springs leaks more easily, and becomes heavy through soaking water.

The wooden canoe is speedy, but its construction makes the finest lines impossible, and fine lines mean more than beauty. They mean seaworthiness and stability and give to a canoe that quality of being alive and intelligent, of meeting waves like conquerors and not like sawlogs.

The canvas canoe, when properly made of the best materials, is the best craft, although many experienced canoemen prefer the wooden variety so commonly used in Canada. The canvas canoe's construction is identical with that of the birch bark, after which it was patterned. It has, however, the advantage of an even, smooth surface, of greater rigidity, of faster lines. It retains its shape and is the superior of both the other types in withstanding hard usage. The well built, intelligently designed canvas canoe is really a wonderful craft. The best stock, careful workmanship, and the results of experiments and experiences have been combined until there is hardly room for improvement. The canvas covering has been rendered almost impervious to ordinary knocks and will often hold water when the planking and ribs have been crushed. If torn, it is easily mended.

The birchbark canoe, built by Indians, is, some things considered, the most wonderful craft of the three. For ten dollars I purchased a sixteen-foot canoe that rode six-foot rollers on Rainy Lake without taking a drop of water. For three dollars I once bought a twelve-foot birch that weighed little more than twenty pounds and never leaked a drop in an entire summer's travel.

But good canoe makers among the Indians are becoming scarce, forest fires have made it difficult to obtain good birch bark, and in many localities Indians are using the white man's canoes when they are able to buy them.

TYPES OF CANOES

Still, a good birchbark is to be had, though much care must be taken in selecting it. As a rule, it is better not to order it made, for the Indian will not do nearly so good a piece of work. Buy a canoe he has made for himself, and be on the ground when you buy it.

Get a canoe of three pieces. That is, a craft made with three separate pieces of birch bark on the bottom. One of two pieces, or of one, will buckle, or bulge, in the center. This greatly retards it. See that the bark is sound and not filled with many tiny holes, that it has been well sewed with the split and skinned roots of jackpine or cedar, that the thwarts and ribs are strong and the planking well placed in position. The planking will slip and expose the bark in a poor canoe.

Many birch canoes will warp and twist. Few are ever perfectly straight. Get one with the bottom, from bow to stern, as flat as possible. Indians have a habit of lifting the ends, thereby making an excellent craft for running rapids, but one almost impossible for the ordinary canoeman on windy lakes.

Treat your bark canoe with consideration, though you will be surprised to discover what hard knocks it will stand without showing a mark. Be specially careful when landing and embarking, keeping it away from rocks and snags. If possible, never get sand in the canoe. This, working down between bark and planking, gradually wears thorugh the bark, a fact which furnishes one of the greatest objections to this style of canoe.

If you have an opportunity to buy a good birch from an Indian, do not care to spend the money a white man's canoe will cost, and are willing to use it carefully, you will have a craft that will keep going when wooden or canvas canoes turn to shore. But you will travel much more slowly with the same expenditure of energy, and you must always carry a can of pitch wedged in the bow. Your craft will be harder to handle, especially in a wind, and, unless you rig some sort of a low thwart or a low seat, you must kneel in the Indian's position when you paddle.

There are several varieties of wooden canoes. In Canada this type has been in constant use for many years. In some districts any canoe, canvas or wooden, made by a white man, is called a " Peterborough," the name of the city in which wooden canoes are extensively built. A woodsman told me, in the summer of 1912, of a wonderful new canoe he had seen a few days before. His enthusiasm led me to expect something marvelous. "It had a lot of wide ribs and was covered all over with painted cloth," he said.

The man, a good woodsman, had never seen or heard of a canvas canoe. In many parts of the United States the wooden canoe of the Canadians is equally unknown.

The most common form of wooden canoe is the basswood. This is made of thin boards of basswood placed over hardwood ribs six inches apart. Strips of hardwood are used to batten the cracks. Ribs and battens are generally rounded and three-quarters of an inch wide.

Another variety is known as the longitudinal strip canoe, made of strips of cedar an inch wide running from end to end and placed over hardwood ribs similar to those in a basswood craft, but closer together. Still another is the cedar rib canoe, made entirely of ribs, with only two or three longitudinal strips besides the gunwales and keel. These ribs, or arches, are one inch wide and fitted together. The last two models are wonderfully strong canoes, though the cedar is not so tough as the basswood. The cost of the rib canoe is far above that of other models, wooden or canvas.

THE CANOE

The cedar types are light. The basswood is when it is new. Both absorb much water, the basswood becoming especially heavy on a portage at the end of a summer which calls for the expenditure of valuable energy.

One great objection to the basswood canoe now generally on the market is that it must be kept in the water. Turned over in the sun for a few hours, it opens up until it is like a sieve. Even when in use in a hot sun the upper seams will open. Dry-kiln lumber is largely responsible. The earlier product was much better. I once saw a basswood canoe that had been in use for twenty-six years.

The construction of the wooden canoe precludes the possibilities of the best lines. I have used wooden canoes that were remarkably seaworthy, but the usual model is not to be compared with a birchbark or canvas. They seem to have a stubborn rigidity that prevents a compromise with a roller.

All wooden canoes of the Canadian model are made without seats. A cross bar or thwart is placed about ten inches above the bottom. This can be used as a seat, but it is not comfortable. The intention is to have the paddlers kneel, as all paddlers should do, resting part of the weight on the thwart and part on the knees. The question of seats and kneeling is discussed in another chapter.

The canvas canoe is simply a birchbark made by a white man, with a white man's tools, with one substituted material made by white men, and with the addition of cane seats. This adherence to the Indian model permits grace and beauty in the lines, valuable, not for the artistic effect, but for the resulting efficiency.

The canoe is made over a solid mold. Ribs two to three inches wide and about a quarter or three-eighths of an inch thick are placed on the mold. The ribs are of cedar. On top are placed thin cedar planks, or strips, generally an eighth of an inch or more thick. The ribs are fastened to gunwales and hardwood stems placed at each end. Over all is stretched tightly a piece of canvas, which is filled with a preparation and given several coats of paint and varnish. The result is a craft identical, in essentials, with the Indian's canoe, only with the canvas taking the place of the birch bark.

However, that is only a simple statement of the construction. Methods, workmanship, efficiency of materials, finishing, and general knowledge of the necessities in construction

THE CANOE

vary so that canoes of all grades are produced. There are canvas canoes whose strength is almost past belief, and there are some on the market that could not stand three hundred miles in northern waters.

But the good canvas canoe, with its solid construction, keeps its shape, offers a smooth surface to the water, is light, is buoyant, will stand very hard knocks and is, all facts considered, the best all around craft.

But much depends upon the construction. The use of clear white cedar is essential. The treatment of the canvas is most important. I have seen a canoe, in the water only two weeks, show cracks and holes due to the action of the sun alone.

The compromise which must be effected between weight and rigidity is delicate, and some makers are prone to one extreme or the other. A sixty-pound canoe, carrying two 150-pound men and one hundred and fifty or two hundred pounds of duffle, is put to severe tests in riding a heavy sea or shooting a twisting, tearing current. I once saw the inwale of a canoe snapped in two when two men were riding terrific waves. There was 170 pounds in each end of the canoe, and nothing in the center. One can readily see the stress and strain that resulted in climbing and pitching over six-foot waves.

The double or open gunwale construction is best for several reasons. Manufacturers will tell you it is stronger. It has the great advantage of permitting a thorough cleaning of the canoe, something almost impossible with the closed gunwales. Sand will get into your craft, and this will work in between the planking and the canvas, as in a birchbark. In time, the threads are worn and cut, and leaks result. With open gunwales the canoe is cleaned every time it is turned over, while a little attention will keep it entirely free from sand.

And right here the canvas canoe has a great advantage over the wooden canoe, especially the basswood craft. It can be taken from the water and turned over in the sun, and, if it is a good canoe, will not be damaged. It is kept dry and light and can be carried out of the wind so that a rising sea cannot touch it.

The planking in a canvas canoe is an important feature. The edges should be matched perfectly, and the strips should run from end to end to give the best rigidity.

The construction of the ribs and the number used is most important. The greater the load a canoe is to carry, and the rougher the water to be traversed, the more rigid must be the ribbing. Some manufacturers, to meet the need for an unusually strong canoe, " double rib " the craft, placing the ribs less than half an inch apart, or build a canoe with "half ribs," which stretch only across the bottom between the full ribs. The usual spacing of the ribs in a well-made canoe is sufficient for all ordinary usage, although it is always advisable to use a floor grating. When ribs are too far apart, or planking is not continuous from bow to stern, the canoe will bend, or "hog," in the center.

The ends should be well protected by brass bang plates which should run well under the canoe. These should be riveted solidly to the stems. Manufacturers will furnish an outside stem of hardwood, which strengthens and protects, but which, like many other things, adds weight.

Some manufacturers place keels on canoes only upon request, as a rule, unless the craft be a large freight model. There is the narrow keel, about an inch deep, which strengthens the canoe and makes handling easier on windy lakes, and the shoe keel, or broad, flat protection for the bottom where rocky river beds are to be passed over. Like the outside stems, they must be considered in the compromise which one must make in the selection of his canoe, and their use or absence depends much on what is to be done with the craft.

The selection of the manufacturer depends on several things. Some sell canoes at much lower prices than others. Perhaps the best general advice is to adapt the price to the use of the canoe. If you are going to Hudson Bay, or Lake Mistisinni, or some other place far from civilization, pay the higher price. But put the money into canoe and not polished trimmings. If you are going to paddle on a small lake or city park lagoon and never leave home, the cheaper canoe will be sufficient. Don't go to the lower extreme, however. The best is none too good where a man's life depends on his canoe. The cheapest doesn't pay, even where only a sunset paddle will be the extent of your canoeing.

CANOE MODELS; THEIR ADAPTABILITY AND USES

IN this chapter the word model applies to the lines, dimensions, and shapes of canoes. There are any number of models, some manufacturers making a dozen or more, while others make only one or two. Canoes are made twelve feet long and twenty-five or thirty. They are made twenty-six inches wide and forty-six or more.

Some canoes are built solely for speed, as the Canadian racing canoe. Others are built for general use but with speed the essential consideration. Some are built for lightness, and others for strength. Most manufacturers try to reach that point where these two qualities meet. Some canoes are wide and "tubby." Others are narrow to the point of crankiness. Some are round bottomed, and others perfectly flat. Some have straight or out-flaring sides, and others have a tumble-home, or outward bulge, of one to two inches.

CANOE MODELS

Some canoes are built for racing, some for paddling in a park lagoon, some for carrying heavy loads, some for running rapids, some for climbing heavy seas in lake travel. Some canoes will weigh from a third to a half as much more than others of the same size. Some will be stiff and heavy and others so pliant they are weak and dangerous.

All these various models are built with a purpose or to try out some freak notion of a designer. I have seen canoes that seem to have been just made, purpose, thought, or possible use never seeming to have entered the head of the builder. But, as a rule, you can find a canoe built for just what you want a canoe to do. It is built for it, but it is not quite the thing, simply because perfection is impossible.

This is essentially true in out of door life. The perfect piece of equipment, tent, cooking utensil, packing contrivance, or whatever you wish, has not been made because, of necessity, everything you take into the wilderness must be a compromise. Your canoe must be a compromise, and it is only in effecting the best possible reconciliation of divergent, contradictory factors that you can approach perfection.

For instance, a canoe suited to running

155

rapids should have the ends raised, the bottom curved from bow to stern, that the craft may be twisted on its center, and that the current may not grip the ends. Such a canoe causes much trouble on windy lakes, for the same factor that makes it easily turned in the rapids makes it hard to keep straight in a wind.

A canoe that has good capacity and stability is slower as the greater beam and blunter bow and stern cut down the speed. A canoe that will rise with a roller, and not cut down through it, is slower than the long, tapered-bow affair. The canoe with a flat bottom is more stable and more buoyant, but it has not the speed of a round-bottomed canoe.

A canoe that is perfectly rigid, made to stand great strains and carry heavy loads, is heavy on a portage, and an extremely light canoe, for the opposite reason, will not stand the strain of a long journey in rough country. A large freight canoe will ride big seas, carry a monster load, and is strong and will stand a lot of hard usage, but it is generally too heavy for one man to carry on a portage.

Thus, your canoe must be selected for the use to which you intend to put it. Length, width, depth, construction, height of ends,

A canvas canoe built especially for use on large, windy lakes, and for carrying heavy loads. Note that the width is carried into the bow and stern not only at the gunwale but in the flat floor.

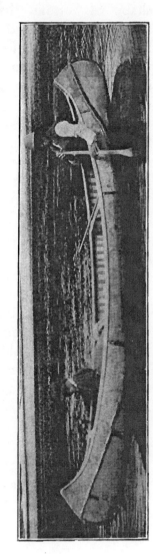

A good canoe for use in rapid-filled rivers. Note that the bottom is much lower in the centre than at the ends. The canoe is easily pivoted, and the curl of rapids will not turn it so quickly.

157

shape of bottom, thwarts, seats, and accessories must be considered carefully. Adapt it as nearly to the use as possible. Balance weight against strength, speed against capacity and stability, weighing the relative value of each quality.

For instance, if two men wish to take a trip down the Nepisiguit or Tobigue rivers, and intend to be in the woods two weeks, they have the following to consider: One hundred and fifty to two hundred pounds should cover food and outfit. There are many rapids. Some they will run and some they will portage around.

They should have a canoe built for river work, a slightly rounded bottom and ends raised higher than the center, on the bottom, for twisting more quickly and more safely in fast water. It should be sixteen feet long and not less than thirty-two inches wide. It should have long, slim ends for speed. The depth should be twelve inches at least. It is not necessary to have much tumble-home. The weight need not be more than sixty-five pounds. Neither can it be much less and still have the craft withstand the wrenching of the rapids and contact with rocks. A shoe keel protects the craft. This is generally half an inch thick and three inches wide in the center, tapering to the ends.

Such a canoe would not do for a trip through western Ontario, where the travel is almost entirely on lakes and where there are few rapids that can be run. If the same two men intend to spend two weeks in such a country they will have the following conditions: Many broad lakes, heavy seas, many portages of varying lengths up to two miles. These demand a flat-bottomed, straight-keeled craft thirteen inches deep and thirty-four inches wide. The ends must not be high enough to catch much wind. Wide outwales help greatly in turning combers. A good tumble home adds stability and also helps keep out the waves. The weight should be between sixty-five and seventy pounds. This will enable them to make a portage in one trip, one taking a heavy pack and the other a light pack and the canoe. The straight bottom is essential in heavy winds. The canoe will not be so apt to turn and bolt. The increased depth is necessary in heavy seas, and a canoe of that weight and size should be strong enough to stand the strain of pitching and tossing.

The width should not all be in the center, but should be carried well into the ends. The blunter bow will aid in riding waves, although it will cut down on the speed.

Consider these two men planning to float down the Ohio, the Mississippi, or some of their tributaries. The length of the trip makes little difference, for supplies may be purchased every day. There are no portages, except possibly around a dam, and then an express wagon will take all their outfit in one trip. They can take all the comforts of home, if they wish, a sheet iron stove, a large tent with dining fly, canned goods and other things with which a sporting goods house catalog is filled.

They can get a seventeen-foot canoe that weighs eighty pounds, for it will not have to be carried, and the larger canoe permits taking a larger outfit. Speed does not count for much, for the current does most of the work. There are no rapids to be run. They may, however, find some ugly seas on these rivers, especially when the wind is against a strong current. For that reason a canoe adapted to lake work, with the width carried well into the ends, a tumble- home, and a depth of thirteen or fourteen inches is best.

This is for down-stream work, however. If the canoe is to be used both up and down stream, it is better to get a faster craft with long tapering ends and keep ashore when the river gets ugly.

But we will imagine these two men are experienced canoemen, that they wish to penetrate the country west of Hudson Bay, or some district far north. They have these conditions: Large lakes, rapid-filled rivers, long, rough portages, the necessity of taking supplies for two or three months.

They want a canoe that will ride seas, and such a canoe can, if necessary, run rapids. So they take the straight-keeled craft and depend upon their skill to handle it in fast water. They will take a sixteen-foot canoe thirteen or fourteen inches deep, thirty or thirty-six inches wide, and of about seventy pounds weight. They will select a good make and pay a good price, for a canoe of that weight must be wonderfully well made to stand the strain to which they will put it. A saving in purchase may cost dear in the end.

They will have a canoe with a good tumble-home and one in which the width and flat floor are carried well into the bow and stern, for both these features increase the carrying capacity and buoyancy and add to the seaworthiness.

With such a craft they can carry three or

four hundred pounds of equipment and food and be able to make good time and live out a good gale. They will not have too much canoe to carry on portages and every pound counts when you are to be gone two or three months. Their craft should withstand rough usage and come back sound as when it started, except for a possible patch or two on the canvas. The necessary supplies for making repairs are mentioned elsewhere.

But if these two men decide to stay at home and paddle about the park lagoon, they do not have to consider capacity, width, weight, rigidity, high ends, and what-not. They want a craft that paddles without much effort, that has quite a bit of speed. They want a canoe that is graceful, with the high ends Indians are supposed to build, and that has a bright coat and shining gunwales and decks. They get a sixteen-foot canoe thirty-one or thirty-two inches wide, with a bottom somewhat rounded and with long, tapering ends. All these factors go for speed and ease in paddling. It will be eleven inches deep, which brings down the weight, adds to the beauty and grace, and is sufficient for the waves they will encounter. It need not have great carrying capacity, for they will never carry more than a basket of lunch. And their canoe, unsuitable for a trip in the wilderness, is as smart a looking craft, and as sufficient for their purpose, as any made.

The following are the essential factors to be remembered in selecting a canoe, it being assumed that the length is sixteen feet:

In quiet waters the depth need be no more than eleven inches. For rivers it should be twelve inches, for lake travel thirteen, and on a long journey, where the load is to be heavy, it should be fourteen.

The width may be thirty-one inches for quiet water and where speed is desired rather than capacity or stability. As greater capacity and stability are required, the width should be increased to thirty-five or thirty-six inches in the center and bow and stern broadened at the bottom and on the gunwales.

For river work the canoe should have the ends raised, the bottom bowing upward from the center, but for lake work the keel should be straight. For heavy lake work a good tumble-home is best, and to get a maximum of seaworthiness and capacity the width should run well into the ends. A rounder bottom gives speed at the sacrifice of stability. A flat bottom gives capacity and stability at the expense of speed, unless the canoe be heavily loaded. Then the flat-bottomed craft is faster.

Have open gunwales that the life of the canvas be prolonged, unless your canoe is to be used at a summer resort for pleasure only, and you use a carpet, pillows, tennis shoes, etc. Then the closed gunwale construction is much neater.

When a canoeman desires to decrease or increase the length of his craft the same general factors should be considered. One man and his pack can travel almost anywhere in a thirteen-foot canoe that should weigh fifty pounds. The depth, for rough travel, should be thirteen inches and the width at least thirty-four. A flat bottom with a good tumble-home will give better stability and capacity, necessary in so short a craft. Such a canoe can carry two men, though the length prohibits dryness in rough water.

The same general factors cover the fourteen and fifteen-foot canoes. A fifteen-foot canoe is suitable for two persons in rough lake travel if the load is not too heavy and if the beam is at least thirty-five inches and the depth thirteen inches.

If three persons intend to use one canoe,

the length should be eighteen feet, though I have made a two weeks' journey on rough lakes with two other persons, complete equipment, and food in a fifteen-foot river model canoe. But it is not advisable. Too much care and exertion in heavy winds are required, the heavy load makes rapid travel too strenuous, and the craft's buoyancy is reduced to such an extent that waves easily come over the bow.

A seventeen-foot canoe, for three persons and equipment, should be thirty-six or thirty-seven inches wide and fourteen inches deep. Every foot you add puts five pounds into a canoe, and, by carrying the width toward the ends, you can get the same capacity in a sixteen-foot canoe as in a seventeen, and so on up. The greater length, on the other hand, gives more room for paddlers and duffle. Such a craft eighteen feet long should be thirty-five inches wide or more and at least thirteen inches deep.

Past the eighteen-foot class one enters the realm of the freight canoe, which may be most anything you wish. For instance, a twenty-foot canoe forty-three or forty-four inches wide and nineteen inches deep will weigh nearly two hundred pounds, but will have a capacity of about 2,500 pounds. The selection of such a canoe should depend upon the amount of freight, the nature of the going, and the efficiency of the canoemen.

Where there are four in a party, however, it is better to use two canoes of sixteen-foot length and suitable to the journey—rivers, lakes, length of trip, etc. Then, if anything happens to one party, there is still a canoe. There is an extra canoe to portage, but a canoe large enough for four would require two men in the portaging, so nothing is lost there. Better time may be made, and each of the four men may paddle more effectively.

It has not been the intention in this chapter to convey the idea that a canoe fit for rivers is unsuitable entirely, or even dangerous, for lakes, and *vice versa*. The object has been to point out the qualities which are essential for an efficient craft in each department of work.

CPSIA information can be obtained at www.ICGtesting.com
Printed in the USA
LVOW12s1759190913

353232LV00001B/172/P